Little Knits for Little Feet

Jody Long

Tuva

Tuva Publishing
www.tuvapublishing.com

Address Merkez Mah. Cavusbasi Cad. No:71
Cekmekoy - Istanbul 34782 / Turkey
Tel: +9 0216 642 62 62

Little Knits For Little Feet

First Print 2016 / December

All Global Copyrights Belong To
Tuva Tekstil ve Yayıncılık Ltd.

Content Knitting

Editor in Chief Ayhan DEMİRPEHLİVAN
Project Editor Kader DEMİRPEHLİVAN
Designer Jody LONG
Technical Editors Leyla ARAS, Büşra ESER
Graphic Designers Ömer ALP, Abdullah BAYRAKÇI
Assistant Zilal ÖNEL
Photograph Tuva Publishing

ISBN: 978-605-5647-69-8

Printing House
Bilnet Matbaacılık ve Ambalaj San. A.Ş.

 TuvaYayincilik TuvaPublishing
 TuvaYayincilik TuvaPublishing

introduction

There is always something special knitting for babies, especially when you know they will have warm and snuggly toes. The booties and shoes in this book have been designed using pure fibres which are soft against delicate skin with the added bonus of being machine washable.

With the rise of baby showers across the world these designs are fast and simple that'll make excellent gifts for any baby arrival. Most of the designs are suitable for boys and girls with a simple switch of color.

There are so many styles to choose from, so there will be something for everyone to knit and enjoy. Some of my favourites are the double grey booties (page 30), stripes socks (page 41) and the cable cuff booties (page 56). Whichever one you choose to knit first will make fantastic gifts and great keepsakes.

This book has been a real delight to work on as I love designing for babies most of all. It allows you to play around with color and adding cute things like buttons and ribbon for that special touch.

The only problem will be deciding which pair to knit first, so get those needles out and make all those little wriggly toes snug and warm!

Happy Knitting!

Jody Long

contents

BABY BOOTIES

 P. 26

P. 30

 P. 34

P. 36

P. 38

P. 41

 P. 44

P. 48

P. 50

P. 52

P. 56

P. 60

 P. 64

 P. 68

 P. 71

 P. 74

 P. 78

P. 81

 P. 84

 P. 87

 P. 90

 P. 94

P. 98

P. 102

 P. 106

 P. 110

P. 114

 P. 118

 P. 122

 P. 126

Equipment

The pattern will tell you at the start what equipment is required to knit the project. The most important purchase is that of the knitting needles. These come in a range of diameters, which are either described in metric millimetres or by one of two sizing systems. Check the pattern carefully and if you are unsure, ask in the store before purchasing. However, the pattern will give a suggested size only to achieve the correct number of stitches and rows in a given distance.

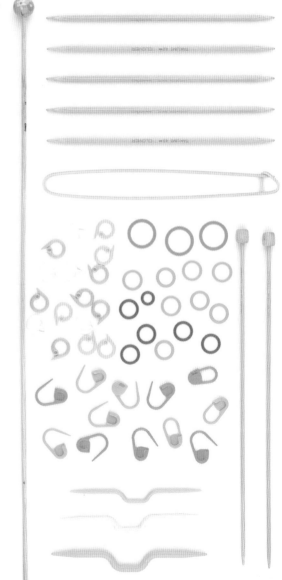

KNITTING NEEDLES

The type used in this book are made from bamboo and are ideal for all types of knitter's because they are light and the stitches are less likely to slide off them than with metal needles.

Check the needles carefully before buying to make sure there is no pitting in the surface and that the points are round and smooth. A longer point is useful on finer sizes. We recommend using Clover knitting needles.

CABLE NEEDLE

This is used for holding stitches to one side while others are being worked within a repeat. Look for a cable needle with a bend in it because it holds the stitches more securely.

STITCH HOLDERS

These prevent stitches from unraveling when not in use. Alternatively, a spare knitting needle of the same size or less (ideally double pointed) can be used as a stitch holder. For holding just a few stitches, a safety pin is always useful.

RULER

A plastic or metal ruler is less likely to become distorted and is useful to check the gauge (tension).

TAPE MEASURE

Useful for greater distances and checking project measurements.

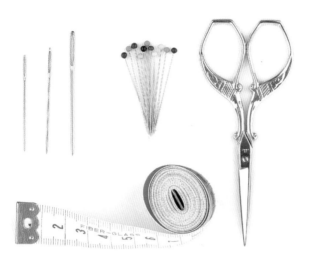

SEWING NEEDLES
These should be blunt and round-pointed with a large eye. A sharp-pointed needle is more likely to split the yarn and/or stitches and result in an uneven seam.

SCISSORS
Always use a nice sharp-pointed pair for easy precise cutting of the yarn.

PINS
Always use large glass/plastic-headed pins so they can be seen and not be left in a knitted garment.

YARN INFORMATION
We have used only natural yarns that are soft against babies skin and most importantly machine washable for busy mums.

Below you will find all the information about the yarns used within this book, both qualities are available in a large color palette.

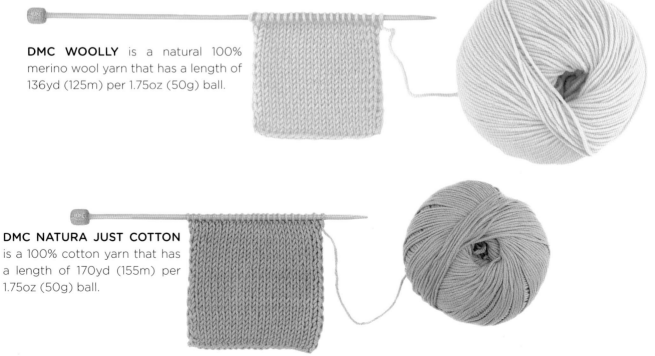

DMC WOOLLY is a natural 100% merino wool yarn that has a length of 136yd (125m) per 1.75oz (50g) ball.

DMC NATURA JUST COTTON is a 100% cotton yarn that has a length of 170yd (155m) per 1.75oz (50g) ball.

Information

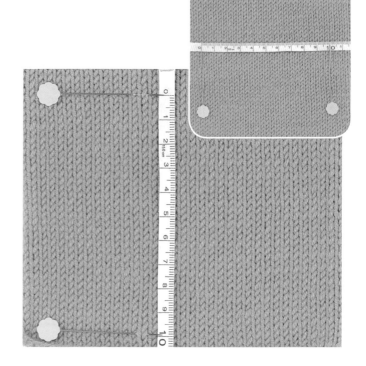

GAUGE (TENSION)

Obtaining the correct tension is perhaps the single factor which can make the difference between a successful garment and a disastrous one. It controls both the shape and size of an article, so any variation, however slight, can distort the finished garment. We recommend that you knit a square in pattern and/or stockinette (stocking) stitch (depending on the pattern instructions) of perhaps 5 - 10 more stitches and 5 - 10 more rows than those given in the tension note.

Mark out the central 4in (10cm) square with pins. If you have too many stitches to 4in (10cm) try again using thicker needles, if you have too few stitches to 4in (10cm) try again using finer needles.

Once you have achieved the correct tension your garment will be knitted to the measurements indicated in the pattern.

CASTING ON

Although there are many different techniques for casting on stitches, we recommend the long-tail cast on method (see page 13) for details.

STOCKINETTE (STOCKING) STITCH

Alternate one row knit and one row purl. The knit side is the right side of the work unless otherwise stated in the instructions.

GARTER STITCH

Knit every row. Both sides are the same and look identical (see page 22).

K1, P1 RIB

Alternate one knit stitch with one purl stitch to the end of the row. On the next row, knit all the knit stitches and purl all the purl stitches as they face you (see page 23).

SEED (MOSS) STITCH

Alternate one knit stitch with one purl stitch to the end of the row. On the next row, knit all the purl stitches and purl and the knit stitches as they face you (see page 23).

INSTRUCTIONS IN ROUNDED BRACKETS

These are to be repeated the number of times stated after the closing bracket.

INSTRUCTIONS IN SQUARE BRACKETS

The instructions are given for the smallest size just before the opening of the bracket. Where they vary, work the figures in brackets for the larger sizes. One set of figures refer to all sizes.

JOINING YARN

Always join yarn at the beginning of a new row (unless you're working the Fair Isle or Intarsia method), and never knot the yarns as the knot may come through to the right side and spoil your work. Any long loose ends will be useful for sewing up afterwards.

WORKING STRIPES

When knitting different-coloured stripes, carry yarns loosely up the side of your work.

FAIR ISLE METHOD

When two or three colours are worked repeatedly across a row, strand the yarn not in use loosely behind the stitches being worked. Always spread the stitches to their correct width to keep them elastic. It is advisable not to carry the stranded or 'floating' yarns over more than three stitches at a time, but weave them under and over the color you are working. The 'floating' yarns are therefore caught at the back of the work.

INTARSIA METHOD

The simplest way to do this is to cut short lengths of yarn for each motif or block of color used in a row. Then joining in the various colors at the appropriate point on the row, link one color to the next by twisting them around each other where they meet on the wrong side of work to avoid leaving a hole. All the ends can then either be darned along the color join lines, as each motif is completed, or they can be 'knitted-in' to the fabric of the knitting as each color is worked into the pattern. This is done in much the same way as 'weaving-in' yarns when working the Fair Isle method and does save time darning-in ends.

WORKING A LACE PATTERN

When working a lace pattern it is important to rememberer that if you are unable to work both the increase and corresponding decrease and vice versa, the stitches should be worked in stockinette (stocking) stitch.

WORKING FROM A CHART

Each square on a chart represents a stitch and a line of squares a row of knitting. Alongside the chart there will be a color and/or stitch key. When working from the charts, read odd rows (knit) from right to left and even rows (purl) from left to right, unless otherwise stated.

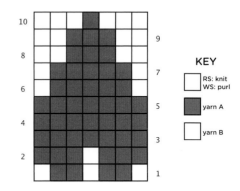

SEAMS

After working for hours knitting a garment, it seems a great pity that many garments are spoiled because such little care is taken in the pressing and finishing process. Follow the text below for a truly professional-looking garment.

PRESSING

Block out each piece of knitting and following the instructions on the ball band press the garment pieces, omitting the ribs. Tip: Take special care to press the edges, as this will make sewing up both easier and neater. If the ball band indicates that the fabric is not to be pressed, then covering the blocked out fabric with a damp white cotton cloth and leave it to stand will have the desired effect. Darn in all loose ends neatly along the selvage edge or a colour join, as appropriate.

STITCHING

When stitching the pieces together, remember to match areas of color and texture very carefully where they meet. Use a seam stitch such as backstitch or mattress stitch for all main knitting seams and join all ribs and cuffs with mattress stitch, unless otherwise stated.

Techniques

HOLDING THE NEEDLES

Not every knitter holds their needles and yarn in the same way. The yarn can be held in either the right or left hand, the needles can be held from above or below. Try each of the methods described here and work in a way that is most comfortable for you. They are all bound to feel awkward and slow at first.

English method
(yarn in the right hand)

Left hand: hold the needle with the stitches in your left hand with your thumb lying along the needle, your index finger resting on top near the tip and the remaining fingers curled under the needle to support it. The thumb and the index finger control the stitches and the tip of the needle.

Right hand: pass the yarn over the index finger, under the middle and over the third finger. The yarn lies between the nail and the first joint and the index finger 'throws' the yarn around the right-hand needle when knitting. The yarn should be able to move freely and is tensioned between the middle and third finger. You can wrap the yarn around the little finger if you feel it is too loose and it keeps falling off your fingers. Hold the empty needle in your right hand with your thumb lying along the needle,

your index finger near the tip and the remaining fingers curled under the needle to support it (see right hand in Continental method).

Some knitters prefer to hold the end of the right-hand needle under their right arm, anchoring it firmly. Whilst knitting this needle remains still and the right hand is above the needle and moves the yarn around it.

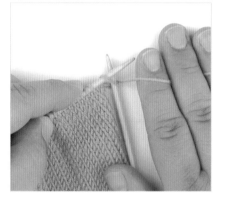

Alternative grip

Left hand: hold the needle in the same way as shown above left.

Right hand: hold the yarn in the fingers the same way as shown above. Hold the needle like a pen, on top of the hand between thumb and index finger. The end of the needle will be above your right arm, in the crook of the elbow. As the fabric grows longer, the thumb will hold the needle behind the knitting.

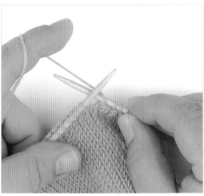

Continental method
(yarn in the left hand)

Left hand: wrap the yarn around your little finger, under the middle two fingers and then over the index finger between the nail and the first joint. The yarn is held taut between the index finger and the needle. Hold the needle with your thumb lying along the needle, your index finger near the tip and remaining fingers curled under the needle to support it. The thumb and index finger control the stitches, yarn and needle tip.

Right hand: hold the empty needle in your right hand with your thumb lying along the needle, index finger resting on top near the tip and remaining fingers curled under the needle to support it. The thumb and index finger control the stitches and the needle tip, which hooks the yarn and draws the loop through.

To begin knitting, you need to work a foundation row of stitches called casting on. There are several ways to cast on depending on the type of edge that you want. The cast on edge should be firm; too loose and it will look untidy and flare out, too tight and it will break and the stitches unravel. If your casting on is always too tight, use a size larger needle. If it is always too loose, use a size smaller needle. Remember to change back to the correct size needle to begin knitting.

Thumb method
This is the simplest way of casting on and you will need only one needle.

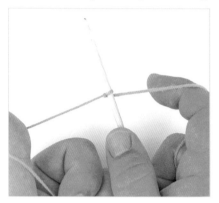

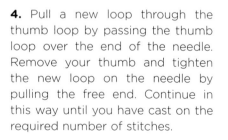

1. Make a slip knot some distance from the end of the yarn (see Knit Perfect) and place it on the needle. Hold the needle in your right hand. Pass the ball end of the yarn over the index finger, under the middle and then over the third finger. Holding the free end of yarn in your left hand, wrap it around your left thumb from front to back.

2. Insert the needle through the thumb loop from front to back.

3. Wrap the ball end over the needle.

The slip knot counts as the first cast on stitch. It is made some distance from the end of the yarn and placed on the needle. Pull the ends of the yarn to tighten it. You now have two ends of yarn coming from the slip knot; the ball end attached to the ball and a shorter free end.

4. Pull a new loop through the thumb loop by passing the thumb loop over the end of the needle. Remove your thumb and tighten the new loop on the needle by pulling the free end. Continue in this way until you have cast on the required number of stitches.

For the thumb method of casting on, you will need approximately 1in (2.5cm) for every stitch you want to cast on. When you have cast on, you should have at least a 6in (15cm) length to sew in.

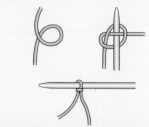

INTRODUCING KNIT STITCH

In knitting there are only two stitches to learn - knit stitch (K) and purl stitch (P). They are the foundation of all knitted fabrics. Once you have mastered these two simple stitches, by combining them in different ways you will soon be knitting ribs, textures, cables and many more exciting fabrics.

English Method (yarn in the right hand)
In knit stitch the yarn is held at the back of the work (the side facing away from you) and is made up of four steps.

1. Hold the needle with the cast on stitches in your left hand, and insert the right-hand needle into the front of the stitch from left to right.

2. Pass the yarn under and around the right-hand needle.

3. Pull the new loop on the right-hand needle through the stitch on the left-hand needle.

4. Slip the stitch off the left-hand needle. One knit stitch is completed.

To continue...
Repeat these four steps for each stitch on the left-hand needle. All the stitches on the left-hand needle will be transferred to the right-hand needle where the new row is formed. At the end of the row, swap the needle with the stitches into your left hand and the empty needle into your right hand, and work the next row in the same way.

BINDING (CASTING) OFF

Bind (cast) off purlwise
To bind (cast) off on a purl row, simply purl the stitches instead of knitting them.

1. Knit two stitches, insert the tip of left-hand needle into the front of the first stitch on the right-hand needle. Lift this stitch over the second stitch and off the needle.

2. One stitch is left on the right-hand needle. Knit the next stitch and lift the second stitch over this and off the needle. Continue in this way until one stitch remains on the right-hand needle.

3. To finish, cut the yarn (leaving a length long enough to sew in), thread the end through the last stitch and slip it off the needle. Pull the yarn end to tighten the stitch and secure.

14

INTRODUCING PURL STITCH

You may find purl stitch a little harder to learn than knit stitch. But really it is just the reverse of a knit stitch. If you purled every row, you would produce garter stitch (the same as if you knitted every row). It is not often that you will work every row in purl stitch; it is easier and faster to knit every row if you want garter stitch.

English method (yarn in the right hand)
In purl stitch the yarn is held at the front of the work (the side facing you) and is made up of four steps.

1. Hold the needle with the cast on stitches in your left hand, and insert the right-hand needle into the front of the stitch from right to left.

2. Pass the yarn over and around the right-hand needle.

3. Pull the new loop on the right-hand needle through the stitch on the left-hand needle.

4. Slip the stitch off the left-hand needle. One stitch is completed.

To continue...
Repeat these four steps for each stitch on the left-hand needle. All the stitches on the left-hand needle will be transferred to the right-hand needle where the new purl row is formed. At the end of the row, swap the needle with the stitches into your left hand and the empty needle into your right hand, and work the next row in the same way.

INCREASING STITCHES

To shape knitting, stitches are increased or decreased. Increases are used to make a piece of knitting wider by adding more stitches, either on the ends of rows or within the knitting. Some increases are worked to be invisible whilst others are meant to be seen and are known as decorative increases. You can increase one stitch at a time or two or more.

Increasing one stitch

The easiest way to increase one stitch is to work into the front and back of the same stitch. This produces a small bar across the second (increase) satitch and is very visible. This makes counting the increases easier.

On a knit row (Kfb)   **On a purl row (Pfb)**

1. Knit into the front of the stitch as usual, do not slip the stitch off the left-hand needle but knit into it again through the back of the loop.

2. Slip the original stitch off the left-hand needle. You have now increased an extra stitch and you can see the bar (increased stitch) to the left of the original stitch.

3. Purl into the front of the stitch as usual, do not slip the stitch off the left-hand needle but purl into it again through the back of the loop.

4. Slip the original stitch off the left-hand needle. You have now increased an extra stitch and you can see the bar (increased stitch) to the left of the original stitch.

To make a neater edge when working increases at the beginning and end of rows, work the increase stitches a few stitches from the end. This leaves a continuous stitch up the edge of the fabric that makes sewing up easier. Because the made stitch lies to the left of the original stitch, at the beginning of a knit row you knit one stitch, then make the increase, but at the end of a knit row you work the increase into the third stitch from the end. The increase stitch lies between the second and third stitches at each end.

On a purl row you work in exactly the same way; the bar will be in the correct position two stitches from either end.

This is another way to increase one stitch and is often used where increasing stitches after a rib. The new stitch is made between two existing stitches using the horizontal thread that lies between the stitches - called the running thread. This is an invisible increase and is harder to see when counting.

On a knit row (M1)

1. Knit to the point where the increase is to be made. Insert the tip of the left-hand needle under the running thread from front to back.

2. Knit this loop through the back to twist it. By twisting the stitch it will prevent leaving a hole appearing where the made stitch is.

3. This completes the increase (M1) and 1 extra stitch was made.

On a purl row (M1P)

To work this increase on a purl row, work as given for the knit way but instead purl into the back of the loop.

Increasing more than one stitch

To increase two stitches simply knit into the front, back and then the front again of the same stitch. When knitting bobbles, you will sometimes make five, six or seven stitches out of one stitch in this way. For example, to make seven stitches the instructions would read (k into front and back of same st) 3 times, then k into front again.

DECREASING STITCHES

Decreasing is used at the ends of rows or within the knitted fabric to reduce the number of stitches being worked on. This means that you can shape your knitted fabric by making it narrower.

Decreasing one stitch

The simplest way to decrease one stitch is to knit or purl two stitches together (K2tog or P2tog). Both of these methods produce the same result on the front (knit side) of the work; the decrease slopes to the right.

Always read how to work a decrease very carefully. Some of them have similar abbreviations with only a slight difference between them.

In patterns the designer may use different abbreviations to those given here. Always check the detailed explanation of abbreviations.

(K2tog or P2tog). Both of these methods produce the same result on the front (knit side) of the work; the decrease slopes to the right.

P2tog on a p row Purl to where the decrease is to be, insert the right-hand needle (as though to purl) through the next two stitches and purl them together as one stitch.

K2tog tbl on a k row Knit to where the decrease is to be, insert the right-hand needle through the back of the next two stitches and knit them together as one stitch.

P2tog tbl on a p row Purl to where the decrease is to be, insert the right-hand needle through the back of the next two stitches and purl them together as one stitch.

Decorative decreasing one stitch purlwise

Sometimes decreases are decorative, especially in lace knitting where they form part of the pattern. Then you have to be aware of whether the decrease slants right or left. Each decrease has an opposite and the two of them are called a pair. There is one way to work the decrease that is the pair to p2tog which slopes to the left when seen on the front (knit side) of the work.

DECORATIVE DECREASING ONE STITCH KNITWISE

There are two ways to work the decrease that is the pair to K2tog. They both produce the same result and slope to the left.

Slip one, slip one, knit two together (SSK)

1. Slip two stitches knitwise one at a time from left-hand needle to right-hand needle.

2. Insert the left-hand needle from left to right through the fronts of these two stitches and knit together as one stitch.

Slip one, knit one, pass slipped stitch over (SKPO)

1. Insert the right-hand needle knitwise into the next stitch.

2. Slip it on to the right-hand needle without knitting it, then knit the next stitch.

3. With the tip of the left-hand needle, lift the slipped stitch over the knitted stitch and off the needle. This is like binding (casting) off one stitch.

Slip two, knit one, pass the two slipped stitches over (SK2PO)

1. Insert the right-hand needle knitwise into the next two stitches as if to knit two stitches together without knitting them, slip the two stitches from left-hand needle to right-hand needle.

2. Knit the next stitch, then with the tip of left-hand needle, lift the two slipped stitches over the knitted stitch and off the needle.

3. You have now completed the central double decrease.

Flat knitting is knitted in rows, working back and forth, moving the stitches from one needle to the other. Circular knitting is knitted in rounds, working round and around without turning the work.

working on four needles

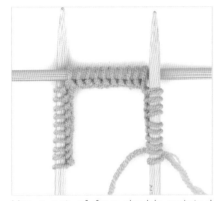

Use a set of four double-pointed needles, adding the stitches at one end and taking them off at the other. Cast the stitches on to one needle and then divide them evenly between three of the needles. For example, if you need to cast on 66 sts, there will be 22 sts on each needle; if you need to cast on 68 sts, there will be 23 sts on two of the needles and 22 on the third. The fourth needle is the working needle.

Knit the stitches from the second needle, then use the new working needle to knit the stitches from the third needle. One round has been completed. Continue in this way, working in rounds and creating a tube of fabric. By knitting each round you will produce stockinette (stocking) stitch. To produce garter stitch, you will need to knit one round and then purl one round.

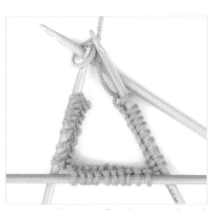

Arrange the needles into a triangle, making sure the cast on edge faces inwards and is not twisted. Place a marker between the last and first cast on stitches to identify the beginning of the round. Slip this marker on every round. Knit the first stitch, pulling up the yarn firmly so there is no gap between the third and first needle. Knit across the rest of the stitches on the first needle. As this needle is now empty, it becomes the working needle.

> The first round is awkward; the needles not being used dangle and get in the way. When you have worked a few rounds the fabric helps hold the needles in shape and knitting will become easier.

> For maximum control, always use the correct length of needle for what you are knitting; short needles for a small number of stitches such as for gloves, and longer needles for garments.

> To avoid a gap at the beginning of the first round, use the tail end of the yarn and the working yarn together to work the first few stitches. Or cast on one extra stitch at the end of the cast on, slip it on to the first needle and knit it together with the first stitch.

> Avoid gaps at the change over between needles by pulling the yarn up tightly, or work a couple of extra stitches from the next needle on each round. This will vary the position of the change over and avoid a ladder of looser stitches forming.

> Double-pointed needles are also used for knitting circles and squares or seamless garments. Use five needles to knit a square, with the stitches divided between the four sides.

ICORD

Icord generally uses somewhere between 3-5 stitches. The icord is a tube knitted in the round with two double-pointed needles.

1. Cast on the number required in the pattern. Note the working yarn is attached to the left stitch. Then slide the stitches to the right end of the double-pointed needle.

2. With the yarn at the back begin knitting the first row.

3. Knit first stitch and pull the yarn tight.

4. Continue knitting across the rest of the row as normal. Tug the work from the bottom after each row to help it to take shape and to even out the tension. Don't turn your work.

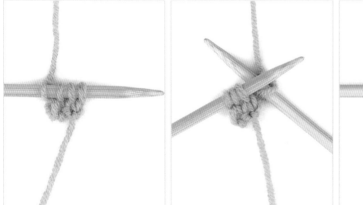

5. Slip the stitches back to the beginning of the double-pointed needle.

6. Knit the second row.

7. Continue in this manner for as long as you need.

8. Pull down on the icord and the gap at the back will close.

GARTER STITCH

Knit every row

When you knit every row the fabric you make is called garter stitch (g st) and has rows of raised ridges on the front and back of the fabric. It looks the same on the back and the front so it is reversible. Garter stitch lies flat, is quite a thick fabric and does not curl at the edges. These qualities make it ideal for borders and collars, as well as for scarves and the main fabric of a garment.

CABLES

Cable knitting always looks more difficult then it actual is. It is simply done by using a cable needle (third needle) to temporarily hold stitches to be transferred to the front or back of your work. Always remember if the cable needle is at the back of work then the cable will lean to the right. If the cable needle is at the front of work then the cable will lean to the left. There are many different cables, always read the instructions and abbreviations carefully as they may look alike or other designers may use different abbreviations. The number of stitches to be moved will be stated in the pattern. Normally cables are worked only on the right side of work, however I have been known to design garments with cables on the wrong side of work too.

Cable front

1. Put the number of stitches stated onto a cable needle.

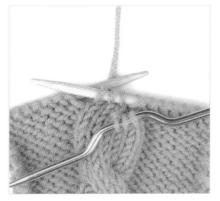

2. Position the cable needle at the front of the work and knit or purl the stated number of stitches from the left-hand needle.

3. Then knit or purl the stated number of stitches from the cable needle.

Cable back

Cable back differs only in that the stitches slipped onto the cable needle are held at the back of the work while the stitches are knitted or purled from the left-hand needle.

INTARSIA

Intarsia is a technique of color knitting used when the color forms blocks within a design. The word intarsia describes the method of securing the blocks of color together. It forms a single layer fabric, which means it is economical with yarn and has a drop similar to a single color fabric. (see page 11) on how to read a chart.

1. Using the color stated in the pattern knit to where the color needs to be changed. Then insert the right-hand needle into the next stitch, and pass the new color under the last color before working the next stitch.

2. The technique is exactly the same for a purl row. The reason you must twisting the yarn colors together as they meet is to avoid leaving a hole.

3. When working a straight color change you will notice you have colored vertical lines on the wrong side of your knitting if you are working the intarsia method correctly. If you work a diagonal color change the colored line where the yarns meet will also run diagonally.

Seed (Moss) stitch

Alternate one knit stitch with one purl stitch to the end of the row. On the next row, knit all the purl stitches and purl and the knit stitches as they face you.

1x1 RIB

Alternate one knit stitch with one purl stitch to the end of the row. On the next row, knit all the knit stitches and purl all the purl stitches as they face you.

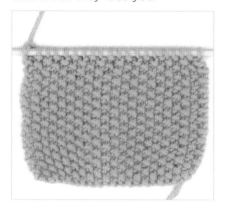

LACE

Simple lace is made up of yarn overs to make a stitch with a pairing decrease to keep the stitch count the same on each row. More complicated lace may have variable stitch counts. No matter which one you are working the rules are the same; If you do not have enough stitches to decrease a yarn over then work this stitch plain and vice versa.

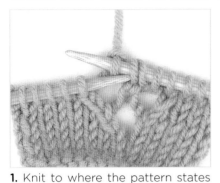

1. Knit to where the pattern states and work a yarn over, by taking the yarn under and over the needle to create a stitch.

2. Work the next two stitches together and work to the end of the row.

3. After working several rows of lace pattern it becomes easier to follow your knitting.

MATTRESS STITCH

This technique produces a discreet seam that is especially good if the edge stitches are not very neat, as they become part of the seam inside the project. The other advantage of mattress stitch is that it is worked from the right side of work, so the neatness of the seam can be assessed as the seam is stitched and adjustments made immediately, rather than having to painstakingly unpick the whole seam. Careful preparation will pay dividends, so press and block the pieces first if required, paying particular attention to the edge stitches. Then pin the seams together and matching pattern if there is any to be matched.

1. Place the edges that need seaming together with right sides of work facing you.

2. Working from the bottom, and between the first and second stitch in from the edge, pass the needle under the loops of two rows on one side; then pass the needle under the loops of the corresponding two rows on other side. Work a few stitches like this before drawing the first stitches tight as this will help to keep track of the line of the seam.

3. The neatest seam is achieved by pulling the yarn just enough to pull the stitches together.

Baby Booties

Garter Stitch Shoe With Chunky Strap

SIZES
0-3 [3-6: 6-9: 9-12] months

ABBREVIATIONS
See inside front flap

MATERIALS NEEDED
🐰 **DMC Woolly** (136 yd/125 m per 50g ball)
1 ball of Pink (042)
🐰 US 3 (3.25 mm) needles
🐰 2 x 18 mm buttons

GAUGE (TENSION)
25 sts and 48 rows to 4 in (10 cm) measured over g st using US 3 (3.25 mm) needles.

LEFT SHOE

Using US 3 (3.25 mm) needles CO 31 [35: 39: 43] sts.

Row 1 (RS): Knit.

Row 2: K1, yo, K14 [16: 18: 20], yo, K1, yo, K14 [16: 18: 20], yo, K1. 35 [39: 43: 47] sts.

Rows 3, 5 and 7: Knit, working K1 tbl into every yo of previous row.

Row 4: K2, yo, K14 [16: 18: 20], yo, K3, yo, K14 [16: 18: 20], yo, K2. 39 [43: 47: 51] sts.

Row 6: K3, yo, K14 [16: 18: 20], yo, K5, yo, K14 [16: 18: 20], yo, K3. 43 [47: 51: 55] sts.

Row 8: K4, yo, K14 [16: 18: 20], yo, K7, yo, K14 [16: 18: 20], yo, K4. 47 [51: 55: 59] sts.

Row 9: Knit, working K1 tbl into every yo of previous row.
Work in g st for 9 [9: 11: 11] rows, ending with RS facing for next row.

Next row: K15 [17: 19: 21], (skpo) 4 times, K1, (K2tog) 4 times, K15 [17: 19: 21]. 39 [43: 47: 51] sts.
Work in g st for 2 rows, ending with **WS** facing for next row. *

Next row (WS): BO 10 [11: 13: 15] sts knitwise (1 st on right needle), K until there are 6 sts on right needle and turn.

Working on these 6 sts only for strap g st 16 rows, ending with RS facing for next row.

Buttonhole row: K1, K2tog, (yo) twice, skpo, K1.

Next row: Knit, working K into front of first yo then K1 tbl into 2nd yo.

Next row: Knit, ending with **WS** facing for next row. BO knitwise (on **WS**).

With RS facing, using US 3 (3.25 mm) needles, rejoin yarn to rem 23 [26: 28: 30] sts and BO knitwise (on **WS**).

RIGHT SHOE

Work as given for left shoe as far as *.

Next row (WS): BO 23 [26: 28: 30] sts knitwise (1 st on right needle), K until there are 6 sts on right needle and turn.

Working on these 6 sts only for strap g st 16 rows, ending with RS facing for next row.

Buttonhole row: K1, K2tog, (yo) twice, skpo, K1.

Next row: Knit, working K into front of first yo then K1 tbl into 2nd yo.

Next row: Knit, ending with **WS** facing for next row. BO knitwise (on **WS**).

With RS facing, using US 3 (3.25 mm) needles, rejoin yarn to rem 10 [11: 13: 15] sts and BO knitwise (on **WS**).

FINISHING

Join row ends and sole edge of each shoe using backstitch or mattress stitch if preferred. Sew on buttons to correspond with buttonholes.

Double Grey Booties

SIZES
0-3 [3-6: 6-9: 9-12] months

ABBREVIATIONS
See inside front flap

SPECIAL ABBREVIATION
K1 below knit into stitch 1 row below

MATERIALS NEEDED
✂ **DMC Woolly** (136 yd/125 m per 50g ball)
1 ball of Light Grey (121) **A**
1 ball of Dark Grey (124) **B**
✂ US 3 (3.25 mm) needles
✂ US 5 (3.75 mm) needles

GAUGE (TENSION)
25 sts and 34 rows to 4 in (10 cm) measured over st st using US 5 (3.75 mm) needles.

LEFT BOOTIE

Using US 5 (3.75 mm) needles and yarn **A** CO 31 [33: 35: 37] sts.

Row 1 (RS): Knit.

Row 2: P1, *K1 below, P1, rep from * to end.
These 2 rows form patt.
Cont in patt for a further 12 [12: 12: 14] rows, ending with RS facing for next row.

Change to US 3 (3.25 mm) needles.

Row 1 (RS): K1, *P1, K1, rep from * to end.

Row 2: P1, *K1, P1, rep from * to end.
These 2 rows form rib.
Cont in rib for a further 5 [5: 5: 7] rows, ending with **WS** facing for next row.

Change to US 5 (3.75 mm) needles and yarn **B**.
Beg with a K row, work in st st for 4 [6: 8: 8] rows, ending with RS facing for next row.

Shape instep

Row 1 (RS): K21 [22: 24: 25], turn.

Row 2: P until there are 11 [11: 13: 13] sts on right needle and turn.

Working on these 11 [11: 13: 13] sts only work as folls:
Beg with a K row, work in st st for 8 [10: 12: 14] rows, ending with RS facing for next row.

Next row (RS): K1, skpo, K to last 3 sts, K2tog, K1.

Next row: Purl.
Rep the last 2 rows once more. 7 [7: 9: 9] sts.
Cut off yarn.

With RS facing, using US 5 (3.75 mm) needles and yarn **B**, rejoin to inner edge of first 10 [11: 11: 12] sts, pick up and knit 8 [10: 12: 14] sts evenly along right side of instep, knit across 7 [7: 9: 9] sts of toe, pick up and knit 8 [10: 12: 14] sts evenly along left side of instep and knit across rem 10 [11: 11: 12] sts. 43 [49: 55: 61] sts.
Work in g st for 5 rows, ending with RS facing for next row.

Shape sole

Row 1 (RS): K1, skpo, K14 [17: 20: 23], K2tog, K5, skpo, K14 [17: 20: 23], K2tog, K1. 39 [45: 51: 57] sts.

Row 2 and every foll alt row: Knit.

Row 3: K1, skpo, K13 [16: 19: 22], K2tog, K3, skpo, K13 [16: 19: 22], K2tog, K1. 35 [41: 47: 53] sts.

Row 5: K1, skpo, K12 [15: 18: 21], K2tog, K1, skpo, K12 [15: 18: 21], K2tog, K1. 31 [37: 43: 49] sts.
Row 7: K1, skpo, K11 [14: 17: 20], sl 1, K2tog, psso, K11 [14: 17: 20], K2tog, K1. 27 [33: 39: 45] sts.

Row 8: Knit.
BO.

RIGHT BOOTIE

Work as given for left bootie.

FINISHING
Join row ends and sole edge of each bootie using backstitch or mattress stitch if preferred, reversing seam for cuff.

Nautical Stripe Booties

SIZES
0-3 [3-6: 6-9: 9-12] months

ABBREVIATIONS
See inside front flap

MATERIALS NEEDED
✂ **DMC Woolly** (136 yd/125 m per 50g ball)
1 ball of Red (052) **A**
1 ball of Navy (076) **B**
1 ball of Cream (003) **C**
✂ US 3 (3.25 mm) needles

GAUGE (TENSION)
28 sts and 36 rows to 4 in (10 cm) measured over st st using US 3 (3.25 mm) needles.

LEFT BOOTIE

Using US 3 (3.25 mm) needles and yarn **A** CO 31 [35: 39: 43] sts.

Rows 1 (RS): Knit.

Row 2: K1, M1, K14 [16: 18: 20], M1, K1, M1, K14 [16: 18: 20], M1, K1. 35 [39: 43: 47] sts.

Row 3 and every foll alt row: Knit.

Row 4: K2, M1, K14 [16: 18: 20], M1, K3, M1, K14 [16: 18: 20], M1, K2. 39 [43: 47: 51] sts.

Row 6: K3, M1, K14 [16: 18: 20], M1, K5, M1, K14 [16: 18: 20], M1, K3. 43 [47: 51: 55] sts.

Row 8: K4, M1, K14 [16: 18: 20], M1, K7, M1, K14 [16: 18: 20], M1, K4. 47 [51: 55: 59] sts.
Cut off yarn **A**.

Shape foot

Row (RS) 1: Using yarn **B** Knit.

Row 2: Using yarn **B** Purl.

Row 3: Using yarn **C** Knit.

Row 4: Using yarn **C** Purl.

Row 5 Using yarn **B** K19 [21: 23: 25], (skpo) twice, K1, (K2tog) twice, K19 [21: 23: 25]. 43 [47: 51: 55] sts.

Row 6: Using yarn **B** Purl.

Row 7: Using yarn **C** K17 [19: 21: 23], (skpo) twice, K1, (K2tog) twice, K17 [19: 21: 23]. 39 [43: 47: 51] sts.

Row 8: Using yarn **C** Purl.

Row 9: Using yarn **B** K15 [17: 19: 21], (skpo) twice, K1, (K2tog) twice, K15 [17: 19: 21]. 35 [39: 43: 47] sts.

Row 10: Using yarn **B** Purl.

Row 11: Using yarn **C** K13 [15: 17: 19], (skpo) twice, K1, (K2tog) twice, K13 [15: 17: 19]. 31 [35: 39: 43] sts.

Row 12: Using yarn **C** Purl.
Keeping the stripes correct, beg with a K row, work in st st for 4 [4: 8: 8] rows without shaping, ending with RS facing for next row.
Using yarn **A** work in g st for 4 rows.

Next 2 rows: Using yarn **C** beg with a K row, work in st st for 2 rows.

Next row: Using yarn **B** Knit.
Using yarn **B** BO knitwise (on **WS**).

RIGHT BOOTIE

Work as given for left bootie.

FINISHING
Join row ends and sole edge of each bootie using backstitch or mattress stitch if preferred.

Two Color Seed Stitch Booties

SIZES
0-3 [3-6: 6-9: 9-12] months

ABBREVIATIONS
See inside front flap

MATERIALS NEEDED
✂ **DMC Woolly** (136 yd/125 m per 50g ball)
1 ball of Yellow (093) **A**
1 ball of Purple (065) **B**
✂ US 5 (3.75 mm) needles
✂ 6 x 15 mm decorative buttons

GAUGE (TENSION)
25 sts and 34 rows to 4 in (10 cm) measured over st st using US 5 (3.75 mm) needles.

LEFT BOOTIE

Using US 5 (3.75 mm) needles and yarn **A** CO 31 [33: 35: 37] sts.

Row 1 (RS): K1, *P1, K1, rep from * to end.
The last row forms seed (moss) st.
Cont in seed (moss) st for a further 17 [17: 19: 21] rows, ending with **WS** facing for next row.

Change to yarn **B**.
Beg with a K row, work in st st for 4 [6: 8: 8] rows, ending with RS facing for next row.

Shape instep

Row 1 (RS): K21 [22: 24: 25], turn.

Row 2: P until there are 11 [11: 13: 13] sts on right needle and turn.
Working on these 11 [11: 13: 13] sts only work as folls:
Beg with a K row, work in st st for 8 [10: 12: 14] rows, ending with RS facing for next row.

Next row (RS): K1, skpo, K to last 3 sts, K2tog, K1.

Next row: Purl.

Rep the last 2 rows once more. 7 [7: 9: 9] sts.
Cut off yarn.

With RS facing, using US 5 (3.75 mm) needles and yarn **B**, rejoin to inner edge of first 10 [11: 11: 12] sts, pick up and knit 8 [10: 12: 14] sts evenly along right side of instep, knit across 7 [7: 9: 9] sts of toe, pick up and knit 8 [10: 12: 14] sts evenly along left side of instep and knit across rem 10 [11: 11: 12] sts. 43 [49: 55: 61] sts.
Next row (WS): Using yarn **B** Knit.
Using yarn **A** work in g st for 2 rows.
Using yarn **B** work in g st for 2 rows.

Shape sole

Row 1 (RS): Using yarn **A** K1, skpo, K14 [17: 20: 23], K2tog, K5, skpo, K14 [17: 20: 23], K2tog, K1. 39 [45: 51: 57] sts.

Row 2: Using yarn **A** Knit.

Row 3: Using yarn B K1, skpo, K13 [16: 19: 22], K2tog, K3, skpo, K13 [16: 19: 22], K2tog, K1. 35 [41: 47: 53] sts.

Row 4: Using yarn **B** Knit.

Row 5: Using yarn **A** K1, skpo, K12 [15: 18: 21], K2tog, K1, skpo, K12 [15: 18: 21], K2tog, K1. 31 [37: 43: 49] sts.

Row 6: Using yarn **A** Knit.

Row 7: Using yarn **B** K1, skpo, K11 [14: 17: 20], sl 1, K2tog, psso, K11 [14: 17: 20], K2tog, K1. 27 [33: 39: 45] sts.

Row 8: Using yarn **B** Knit.
Using yarn **B** BO.

RIGHT BOOTIE

Work as given for left bootie.

FINISHING
Join row ends and sole edge of each bootie using backstitch or mattress stitch if preferred, reversing seam for cuff. Sew on 3 buttons to the front of each bootie as illustrated in photograph.

Rainbow Booties

SIZES
0-3 [3-6: 6-9: 9-12] months

ABBREVIATIONS
See inside front flap

MATERIALS NEEDED
🧶 **DMC Woolly** (136 yd/125 m per 50g ball)
1 ball of Blue (075) **A**
1 ball of Red (052) **B**
1 ball of Orange (102) **C**
1 ball of Yellow (093) **D**
1 ball of Green (081) **E**
🧶 US 3 (3.25 mm) needles
🧶 US 5 (3.75 mm) needles

GAUGE (TENSION)
25 sts and 34 rows to 4 in (10 cm) measured over st st using US 5 (3.75 mm) needles.

LEFT BOOTIE

Using US 3 (3.25 mm) needles and yarn **A** CO 34 [34: 38: 38] sts.

Rows 1 (RS): K2, *P2, K2, rep from * to end.

Row 2: P2, *K2, P2, rep from * to end.
These 2 rows form rib.
Cont in rib for a further 15 [15: 17: 17] rows, dec 3 [1: 3: 1] sts evenly across last row and ending with WS facing for next row. 31 [33: 35: 37] sts.
Beg with a K row, work in st st for 4 [6: 8: 8] rows, ending with RS facing for next row.

Shape instep

Row 1 (RS): K21 [22: 24: 25], turn.

Row 2: P until there are 11 [11: 13: 13] sts on right needle and turn.
Working on these 11 [11: 13: 13] sts only work as folls:

Rows 1 and 2: Using yarn **B** beg with a K row, work in st st.

Rows 3 and 4: Using yarn **C** beg with a K row, work in st st.

Rows 5 and 6: Using yarn **D** beg with a K row, work in st st.

Rows 7 and 8: Using yarn **E** beg with a K row, work in st st.

0-3 [3-6] months only

Row 1 (RS): Using yarn **A** K1, skpo, K to last 3 sts, K2tog, K1. 9 sts.

Row 2: Using yarn **A** Purl.

Row 3: Using yarn **B** K1, skpo, K to last 3 sts, K2tog, K1. 7 sts.

Row 4: Using yarn **B** Purl.
Cut off yarns.

[6-9: 9-12] months only

Rows 1 and 2: Using yarn **A** st st.

Row 3: Using yarn **B** K1, skpo, K to last 3 sts, K2tog, K1. 11 sts.

Row 4: Using yarn **B** Purl.

Row 5: Using yarn **C** K1, skpo, K to last 3 sts, K2tog, K1. 9 sts.

Row 6: Using yarn **C** Purl.
Cut off yarns.

All sizes

With RS facing, using US 5 (3.75 mm) needles and yarn **A**, rejoin to inner edge of first 10 [11: 11: 12] sts, pick up and knit 8 [10: 12: 14] sts evenly along right side of instep, knit across 7 [7: 9: 9] sts of toe, pick up and knit 8 [10: 12: 14] sts evenly along left side of instep and Knit across rem 10 [11: 11: 12] sts. 43 [49: 55: 61] sts.

Work in g st for 5 rows, ending with RS facing for next row.

Shape sole

Row 1 (RS): K1, skpo, K14 [17: 20: 23], K2tog, K5, skpo, K14 [17: 20: 23], K2tog, K1. 39 [45: 51: 57] sts.

Row 2 and every foll alt row: Knit.

Row 3: K1, skpo, K13 [16: 19: 22], K2tog, K3, skpo, K13 [16: 19. 22], K2tog, K1. 35 [41: 47: 53] sts.

Row 5: K1, skpo, K12 [15: 18: 21], K2tog, K1, skpo, K12 [15: 18: 21], K2tog, K1. 31 [37: 43: 49] sts.

Row 7: K1, skpo, K11 [14: 17: 20], sl 1, K2tog, psso, K11 [14: 17: 20], K2tog, K1. 27 [33: 39: 45] sts.

Row 8: Knit.
BO for.

RIGHT BOOTIE

Work as given for left bootie.

FINISHING

Join row ends and sole edge of each bootie using backstitch or mattress stitch if preferred, reversing seam for cuff.

Stripy Socks

SIZES
0-6 [6-12] months

ABBREVIATIONS
See inside front flap

MATERIALS NEEDED
✄ **DMC Woolly** (136 yd/125 m per 50g ball)
1 ball of Green (084) **A**
1 ball of Navy (076) **B**
1 ball of Teal (077) **C**
✄ US 3 (3.25 mm) needles
✄ US 5 (3.75 mm) needles
✄ Stitch holders

GAUGE (TENSION)
25 sts and 34 rows to 4 in (10 cm) measured over st st using US 5 (3.75 mm) needles.

LEFT SOCK

Using US 3 (3.25 mm) needles and yarn **A** CO 27 [33] sts **loosely**.
Change to yarn **B**.

Row 1 (RS): K1, *P1, K1, rep from * to end.

Row 2: P1, *K1, P1, rep from * to end.
These 2 rows form rib.
Cont in rib for a further 4 rows, dec 1 st at end of last row and ending with RS facing for next row. 26 [32] sts.

Change to US 5 (3.75 mm) needles and work as folls:

Rows 1 and 2: Using yarn **B** beg with a K row, work in st st.

Rows 3 and 4: Using yarn **C** g st.

Rows 5 and 6: As rows 1 and 2.

Rows 7 and 8: Using yarn **A** g st.
These 8 rows form stripe patt.
Cont in stripe patt for a further 4 [8] rows, ending with RS facing for next row.

Divide sts for heel

Row 1 (RS): Sl first 7 [9] sts on a holder, using yarn **B** knit 12 [14], slip these 12 [14] sts on a second holder for instep, using yarn **B** knit the rem 7 [9] sts on left needle then knit across the 7 [9] sts from first holder. 14 [18] sts.

Working on these 14 [18] sts only for heel and yarn **B** beg with a P row, work 5 [7] rows in st st, ending with RS facing for next row.

Turn heel

Row 1 (RS): K8 [10], skpo, turn.

Row 2: sl 1, P2, P2tog, turn.

Row 3: sl 1, K3, skpo, turn.

Row 4: sl 1, P4, P2tog, turn.

Row 5: sl 1, K5, skpo, turn.

0-6 months only

Row 6 (WS): sl 1, P6, P2tog. 8 sts.

[6-12] months only

Row 6 (WS): sl 1, P6, P2tog, turn. 10 sts.

Row 7: sl 1, K7, skpo, turn. 9 sts.

Row 8: sl 1, P8, P2tog. 8 sts.

For all sizes

Cut off yarn and sl these rem 8 sts on a holder.
With RS facing, using US 5 (3.75 mm) needles and yarn **B**, pick up and knit 6 [8] sts along side of heel, knit across 8 sts on holder, then pick up and knit 6 [8] sts along other side of heel. 20 [24] sts.

Next row (WS): Purl.

Shape sole

Row 1 (RS): Using yarn **A** [**C**], K1 skpo, K to last 3 sts, K2tog, K1. 18 [22] sts.

Row 2: Using yarn **A** [**C**] knit.
Keeping stripe patt correct, dec 1 st at each end as before on next and every foll alt row until 12 [14] sts rem, then work 11 [13] rows straight thus ending with 2 rows in yarn **A**.
Cut off yarn **A** and **C**.

Shape toe

Using yarn **B** only.

Row 1 (RS): K1, skpo, K to last 3 sts, K2tog, K1. 10 [12] sts.

Row 2: Purl.
Rep last 2 rows until 6 [8] sts rem, ending with RS facing for next row.
BO.

Instep

With **WS** facing, using US 5 (3.75 mm) needles and yarn **B**, purl across 12 [14] sts left on a holder.
Keeping stripe patt correct, work 18 [22] rows straight, ending with RS facing for next row.
Cut off yarn **A** and **C**.

Shape toe

Using yarn **B** only.

Row 1 (RS): K1, skpo, K to last 3 sts, K2tog, K1. 10 [12] sts.

Row 2: Purl.
Rep last 2 rows until 6 [8] sts rem, ending with RS facing for next row.
BO.

RIGHT SOCK

Work as given for left sock.

FINISHING

Join row ends at back, side edges then across toe edge using backstitch or mattress stitch if preferred, taking care to match patt.

Puppy Booties

SIZES
0-3 [3-6: 6-9: 9-12] months

ABBREVIATIONS
See inside front flap

MATERIALS NEEDED
🧶 **DMC Woolly** (136 yd/125 m per 50g ball)
1 ball of Light Brown (110) **A**
1 ball of Dark Brown (116) **B**
🧶 US 3 (3.25 mm) needles
🧶 US 5 (3.75 mm) needles

GAUGE (TENSION)
25 sts and 34 rows to 4 in (10 cm) measured over st st using US 5 (3.75 mm) needles.

LEFT BOOTIE

Using US 3 (3.25 mm) needles and yarn **A** CO 31 [35: 39: 43] sts.

Rows 1 (RS): K1, *P1, K1, rep from * to end.

Row 2: P1, *K1, P1, rep from * to end.
These 2 rows form rib.
Cont in rib for a further 19 [19: 21: 23] rows, ending with **WS** facing for next row.

Change to US 5 (3.75 mm) needles.
Beg with a K row, work in st st for 4 [4: 6: 8] rows, ending with RS facing for next row.

Shape instep

Row 1 (RS): K20 [23: 26: 29], turn.

Row 2: P until there are 9 [11: 13: 15] sts on right needle and turn.
Working on these 9 [11: 13: 15] sts only work as folls:
Beg with a K row, work in st st for 14 [16: 18: 20] rows, ending with RS facing for next row.
Cut off yarn.

With RS facing, using US 5 (3.75 mm) needles and yarn **A**, rejoin to inner edge of first 11 [12: 13: 14] sts, pick up and knit 9 [10: 11: 12] sts evenly along right side of instep, knit across 9 [11: 13: 15] sts of toe, pick up and

knit 9 [10: 11: 12] sts evenly along left side of instep and Knit across rem 11 [12: 13: 14] sts. 49 [55: 61: 67] sts.
Beg with a P row, work in st st for 9 [9: 11: 13] rows, ending with RS facing for next row.
Cut off yarn.

Shape sole

Change to yarn **B**.
Work in g st for 2 rows.

Row 1 (RS): K1, skpo, K18 [21: 24: 27], K2tog, K3, skpo, K18 [21: 24: 27], K2tog, K1. 45 [51: 57: 63] sts.

Row 2: Knit.

Row 3: K1, skpo, K16 [19: 22: 25], K2tog, K3, skpo, K16 [19: 22: 25], K2tog, K1. 41 [47: 53: 59] sts.

Row 4: K1, skpo, K14 [17: 20: 23], K2tog, K3, skpo, K14 [17: 20: 23], K2tog, K1. 37 [43: 49: 55] sts.

[3-6: 6-9: 9-12] months only
Next row: K1, skpo, K— [15: 18: 21], K2tog, K3, skpo, K— [15: 18: 21], K2tog, K1. — [39: 45: 51] sts.

[6-9: 9-12] months only
Next row: K1, skpo, K— [—: 16: 19], K2tog, K3, skpo, K— [—: 16: 19], K2tog, K1. — [—: 41: 47] sts.

[9-12] months only
Next row: K1, skpo, K— [—: —: 17], K2tog, K3, skpo, K— [—: —: 17], K2tog, K1. — [—: —: 43] sts.

For all sizes

Next row: Knit.
BO.

RIGHT BOOTIE

Work as given for left bootie.

EARS (make 4)

Using US 3 (3.25 mm) needles and yarn **A** CO 3 sts for lower edge.
Working in g st throughout **at the same time** inc 1 st at each end of next 3 [3: 4: 4] rows. 9 [9: 11: 11] sts.
Work 5 [5: 6: 6] rows, ending with RS facing for next row.

Dec 1 st at each end of next and every foll 4th row until 3 sts rem.

Work 1 row, ending with RS facing for next row.
BO for top edge.

FINISHING

Join row ends and sole edge of each bootie using backstitch or mattress stitch if preferred, reversing seam for cuff.
Pin BO edge of ear to top of instep as shown. Sew as pinned. Work the other ear in the same manner on the opposite side of instep. Using yarn **B** work facial features by working straight stitches as shown on front of instep. Work the other bootie to match.

Lilac Lace Booties

SIZES
0-6 [6-12] months

ABBREVIATIONS
See inside front flap

MATERIALS NEEDED
✄ **DMC Woolly** (136 yd/125 m per 50g ball)
1 ball of Dark Lilac (062) **A**
1 ball of Light Lilac (061) **B**
✄ US 6 (4 mm) needles
✄ 1yd (90 cm) of 5mm ribbon

GAUGE (TENSION)
23 sts and 29 rows to 4 in (10 cm) measured over st st using US 6 (4 mm) needles.

LEFT BOOTIE

Using US 6 (4 mm) needles and yarn **A** CO 25 [29] sts.

Row 1 (RS): K1, Kfb, K9 [11], Kfb, K1, Kfb, K9 [11], Kfb, K1. 29 [33] sts.

Rows 2 and 4: Purl.

Row 3: K1, Kfb, K11 [13], Kfb, K1, Kfb, K11 [13], Kfb, K1. 33 [37] sts.

Row 5: K1, Kfb, K13 [15], Kfb, K1, Kfb, K13 [15], Kfb, K1. 37 [41] sts.

Row 6: Knit.

Rows 7 and 8: Beg with a K row, work in st st.

**Change to yarn B.
Work in g st for 2 rows.

Row 1 (RS): K1, *yo, K2tog, rep from * to end.

Row 2: Knit.
Change to yarn **A**.

Beg with a K row, work 2 [4] rows in st st, ending with RS facing for next row. **
Rep from ** to ** once more.

Row 1 (RS): (K1, skpo, K13 [15], K2tog) twice, K1. 33 [37] sts.

Row 2 and every foll alt row: Knit.

Row 3: (K1, skpo, K11 [13], K2tog) twice, K1. 29 [33] sts.

Row 5: (K1, skpo, K9 [11], K2tog) twice, K1. 25 [29] sts.

Row 6: Knit.

Ribbon row: K1, *K2tog, yo, K2, rep from * to end.
Beg with a K row, work 6 rows in st st.

Next 2 rows: Purl.

Next 2 rows: Beg with a K row, work in st st.
Change to yarn **B**.
Work in g st for 2 rows.

Next row (RS): K1, *yo, K2tog, rep from * to end.
BO knitwise (on **WS**).

RIGHT BOOTIE

Work as given for left bootie.

FINISHING
Join row ends and sole edge of each bootie using backstitch or mattress stitch if preferred, reversing seam for cuff.
Work the other bootie to match. Cut the length of ribbon in half and thread through ribbon row. Trim to size if required and tie into a bow at front as shown.

Fringe Booties

SIZES
0-3 [3-6: 6-9: 9-12] months

ABBREVIATIONS
See inside front flap

SPECIAL ABBREVIATION
Fringe 1 CO 5 sts onto left needle using the two-needle method, then BO 5 sts (1 st on right needle after BO).

MATERIALS NEEDED
✎ **DMC Woolly** (136 yd/125 m per 50g ball)
1 ball of Light Lime (092)
✎ US 3 (3.25 mm) needles
✎ US 5 (3.75 mm) needles

GAUGE (TENSION)
25 sts and 34 rows to 4 in (10 cm) measured over st st using US 5 (3.75 mm) needles.

LEFT BOOTIE

Using US 3 (3.25 mm) needles CO 31 [33: 35: 37] sts.

Row 1 (RS): K3 [4: 1: 2], fringe 1, *K3, fringe 1, rep from * to last 3 [4: 1: 2] sts, K3 [4: 1: 2].

Row 2: Knit.

Row 3: K1 [2: 3: 4], fringe 1, *K3, fringe 1, rep from * to last 1 [2: 3: 4] sts, K1 [2: 3: 4].

Row 4: Knit.
These 4 rows form patt.
Cont in patt for a further 8 [8: 10: 10] rows, ending with RS facing for next row.

Row 1 (RS): K1, *P1, K1, rep from * to end.

Row 2: P1, *K1, P1, rep from * to end.
These 2 rows form rib.
Cont in rib for a further 9 [9: 11: 11] rows, ending with **WS** facing for next row.

Change to US 5 (3.75 mm) needles.
Beg with a K row, work in st st for 4 [6: 8: 8] rows, ending with RS facing for next row.

Shape instep

Row 1 (RS): K21 [22: 24: 25], turn.

Row 2: P until there are 11 [11: 13: 13] sts on right needle and turn.
Working on these 11 [11: 13: 13] sts only work as folls:
Beg with a K row, work in st st for 8 [10: 12: 14] rows, ending with RS facing for next row.

Next row (RS): K1, skpo, K to last 3 sts, K2tog, K1.

Next row: Purl.
Rep the last 2 rows once more. 7 [7: 9: 9] sts.
Cut off yarn.

With RS facing, using US 5 (3.75 mm) needles, rejoin to inner edge of first 10 [11: 11: 12] sts, pick up and knit 8 [10: 12: 14] sts evenly along right side of instep, knit across 7 [7: 9: 9] sts of toe, pick up and knit 8 [10: 12: 14] sts evenly along left side of instep and Knit across rem 10 [11: 11: 12] sts. 43 [49: 55: 61] sts.
Work in g st for 5 rows, ending with RS facing for next row.

Shape sole

Row 1 (RS): K1, skpo, K14 [17: 20: 23], K2tog, K5, skpo, K14 [17: 20: 23], K2tog, K1. 39 [45: 51: 57] sts.

Row 2 and every foll alt row: Knit.

Row 3: K1, skpo, K13 [16: 19: 22], K2tog, K3, skpo, K13 [16: 19: 22], K2tog, K1. 35 [41: 47: 53] sts.

Row 5: K1, skpo, K12 [15: 18: 21], K2tog, K1, skpo, K12 [15: 18: 21], K2tog, K1. 31 [37: 43: 49] sts.

Row 7: K1, skpo, K11 [14: 17: 20], sl 1, K2tog, psso, K11 [14: 17: 20], K2tog, K1. 27 [33: 39: 45] sts.

Row 8: Knit.
BO.

RIGHT BOOTIE

Work as given for left bootie.

FINISHING
Join row ends and sole edge of each bootie using backstitch or mattress stitch if preferred, reversing seam for cuff.

Bobble Booties

SIZES
0-3 [3-6: 6-9: 9-12] months

ABBREVIATIONS
See inside front flap

SPECIAL ABBREVIATION
MB K into front, back and front again of next st, turn, P3, turn, K3, turn, P3, turn, sl 1, K2tog, psso.

MATERIALS NEEDED
- **DMC Woolly** (136 yd/125 m per 50g ball)
1 ball of Light Pink (041)
- US 3 (3.25 mm) needles
- US 5 (3.75 mm) needles

GAUGE (TENSION)
25 sts and 34 rows to 4 in (10 cm) measured over st st using US 5 (3.75 mm) needles.

LEFT BOOTIE

Using US 5 (3.75 mm) needles CO 31 [33: 35: 37] sts.

Rows 1 and 2: Work in g st.

Row 3: Knit.

Row 4 and every foll alt row: Purl.

Row 5: K3 [4: 1: 2], MB, *K3, MB, rep from * to last 3 [4: 1: 2] sts, K3 [4: 1: 2].

Row 7: K1 [2: 3: 4], MB, *K3, MB, rep from * to last 1 [2: 3: 4] sts, K1 [2: 3: 4].

Row 9: As row 5.

Row 10: Purl.

Rows 11 and 12: As rows 1 and 2.

Change to US 3 (3.25 mm) needles.

Row 1 (RS): K1, *P1, K1, rep from * to end.

Row 2: P1, *K1, P1, rep from * to end.
These 2 rows form rib.
Cont in rib for a further 11 rows, ending with **WS** facing for next row.

Change to US 5 (3.75 mm) needles.
Beg with a K row, work in st st for 4 [6: 8: 8] rows, ending with RS facing for next row.

Shape instep

Row 1 (RS): K21 [22: 24: 25], turn.

Row 2: P until there are 11 [11: 13: 13] sts on right needle and turn.
Working on these 11 [11: 13: 13] sts only work as folls:
Beg with a K row, work in st st for 2 [4: 6: 8] rows, ending with RS facing for next row.

Row 1 (RS): K5 [5: 6: 6], MB, K5 [5: 6: 6].

Row 2 and every foll alt row: Purl.

Row 3: K3 [3: 4: 4], MB, K3, MB, K3 [3: 4: 4].

Row 5: As row 1.

Row 6: Purl.

Next row (RS): K1, skpo, K to last 3 sts, K2tog, K1.

Next row: Purl.
Rep the last 2 rows once more. 7 [7: 9: 9] sts.
Cut off yarn.

With RS facing, using US 5 (3.75 mm) needles, rejoin to inner edge of first 10 [11: 11: 12] sts, pick up and knit 8 [10: 12: 14] sts evenly along right side of instep, knit across 7 [7: 9: 9] sts of toe, pick up and knit 8 [10: 12: 14] sts evenly along left side of instep and Knit across rem 10 [11: 11: 12] sts. 43 [49: 55: 61] sts.
Work in g st for 5 rows, ending with RS facing for next row.

Shape sole

Row 1 (RS): K1, skpo, K14 [17: 20: 23], K2tog, K5, skpo, K14 [17: 20: 23], K2tog, K1. 39 [45: 51: 57] sts.

Rows 2, 4 and 6: Knit.

Row 3: K1, skpo, K13 [16: 19: 22], K2tog, K3, skpo, K13 [16: 19: 22], K2tog, K1. 35 [41: 47: 53] sts.

Row 5: K1, skpo, K12 [15: 18: 21], K2tog, K1, skpo, K12 [15: 18: 21], K2tog, K1. 31 [37: 43: 49] sts.

Row 7: K1, skpo, K11 [14: 17: 20], sl 1, K2tog, psso, K11 [14: 17: 20], K2tog, K1. 27 [33: 39: 45] sts.

Row 8: Knit.
BO.

RIGHT BOOTIE

Work as given for left bootie.

FINISHING

Join row ends and sole edge of each bootie using backstitch or mattress stitch if preferred, reversing seam for cuff.

Cable Cuff Booties

SIZES
0-6 [6-12] months

ABBREVIATIONS
See inside front flap

SPECIAL ABBREVIATION
C4F slip next 2 sts onto CN and leave at front of work, K2, then K2 from CN.

MATERIALS NEEDED
🧶 **DMC Woolly** (136 yd/125 m per 50g ball)
1 ball of Lime (084)
🧶 US 3 (3.25 mm) needles
🧶 US 5 (3.75 mm) needles
🧶 Cable needle

GAUGE (TENSION)
25 sts and 34 rows to 4 in (10 cm) measured over st st using US 5 (3.75 mm) needles.

LEFT BOOTIE

Using US 5 (3.75 mm) needles CO 38 [44] sts.

Row 1 (RS): *P2, K4, rep from * to last 2 sts, P2.

Row 2: *K2, P4, rep from * to last 2 sts, K2.

Row 3: *P2, C4F, rep from * to last 2 sts, P2.

Row 4: As row 2.

These 4 rows form patt.
Cont in patt for a further 8 rows, ending with RS facing for next row.

Next row: Purl, dec 7 [9] sts evenly across row. 31 [35] sts.

Change to US 3 (3.25 mm) needles.

Row 1 (RS): K1, *P1, K1, rep from * to end.

Row 2: P1, *K1, P1, rep from * to end.
These 2 rows form rib.
Cont in rib for a further 10 rows, ending with **WS** facing for next row.

Change to US 5 (3.75 mm) needles.

Next row (RS): K12 [14], P2, K1, Kfb, K1, P2, K12 [14]. 32 [36] sts.

Rows 1 and 3: P12 [14], K2, P4, K2, P12 [14].

Row 2: K12 [14], P2, C4F, P2, K12 [14].

Row 4: K12 [14], P2, K4, P2, K12 [14].
These 4 rows form patt.
Cont in patt for a further 3 [7] rows, ending with RS facing for next row.

Shape instep

Row 1 (RS): K12 [14], P2, K4, P2, K2 [3], turn.

Row 2: P2 [3], K2, P4, K2, P2 [3], there are 12 [14] sts on right needle and turn.
Working on these 12 [14] sts only work as folls:

Row 1 (RS): K2 [3], P2, C4F, P2, K2 [3].

Row 2: P2 [3], K2, P4, K2, P2 [3].

Row 3: K2 [3], P2, K4, P2, K2 [3].

Row 4: As row 2.

These 4 rows form patt.
Cont in patt for a further 4 [8] rows, ending with RS facing for next row.

0-6 months only

Row 1 (RS): K1, skpo, P1, C4F, P1, K2tog, K1. 10 sts.

Row 2: P2, K1, P4, K1, P2.

Row 3: K1, skpo, K4, K2tog, K1. 8 sts.

Row 4: P3, P2tog, P3. 7 sts.
Cut off yarn.

[6-12] months only

Row 1 (RS): K1, skpo, P2, C4F, P2, K2tog, K1. 12 sts.

Row 2: P2, K2, P4, K2, P2.
Row 3: K1, skpo, P1, K4, P1, K2tog, K1. 10 sts.

Row 4: P2, K1, P1, P2tog, P1, K1, P2. 9 sts.
Cut off yarn.

With RS facing, using US 5 (3.75 mm) needles, rejoin to inner edge of first 10 [11] sts, pick up and knit 8 [12] sts evenly along right side of instep, knit across 7 [9] sts of toe, pick up and knit 8 [12] sts evenly along left side of instep and Knit across rem 10 [11] sts. 43 [55] sts.
Work in g st for 5 rows, ending with RS facing for next row.

Shape foot

Row 1 (RS): K1, skpo, K14 [20], K2tog, K5, skpo, K14 [20], K2tog, K1. 39 [51] sts.

Row 2 and every foll alt row: Knit.

Row 3: K1, skpo, K13 [19], K2tog, K3, skpo, K13 [19], K2tog, K1. 35 [47] sts.

Row 5: K1, skpo, K12 [18], K2tog, K1, skpo, K12 [18], K2tog, K1. 31 [43] sts.

Row 7: K1, skpo, K11 [17], sl 1, K2tog, psso, K11 [17], K2tog, K1. 27 [39] sts.

Row 8: Knit.
BO.

RIGHT BOOTIE

Work as given for left bootie.

FINISHING
Join row ends and sole edge of each bootie using backstitch or mattress stitch if preferred, reversing seam for cuff.

Love Heart Lace Booties

SIZES
0-3 [3-6: 6-9: 9-12] months

ABBREVIATIONS
See inside front flap

MATERIALS NEEDED
✤ **DMC Woolly** (136 yd/125 m per 50g ball)
1 ball of Red (051) **A**
1 ball of Cream (003) **B**
✤ US 5 (3.75 mm) needles
✤ 1yd (90 cm) of 5mm ribbon

GAUGE (TENSION)
25 sts and 34 rows to 4 in (10 cm) measured over st st using US 5 (3.75 mm) needles.

LEFT BOOTIE

Using US 5 (3.75 mm) needles and yarn **A** CO 31 [33: 35: 37] sts **loosely**.
Cut off yarn **A**.

Change to yarn **B**.

Row 1 (RS): K1 [2: 3: 1], (yo, skpo, K1) 0 [0: 0: 1] times, *K2tog, yo, K1, yo, skpo, K1, rep from * to last 0 [1: 2: 3] sts, (K2tog, yo) 0 [0: 0: 1] times, K0 [1: 2: 1].

Row 2: Purl.
These 2 rows form patt.
Cont in patt for a further 12 [14: 16: 18] rows, ending with RS facing for next row.
Beg with a K row, work in st st for 2 rows, ending with RS facing for next row.

Shape instep

Row 1 (RS): K21 [22: 24: 25], turn.

Row 2: P until there are 11 [11: 13: 13] sts on right needle and turn.

Working on these 11 [11: 13: 13] sts only work as folls:
Beg with a K row, work in st st for 0 [0: 2: 2] rows, ending with RS facing for next row.

Place chart

Using the **intarsia** technique as described on page 11, now place chart, which is worked entirely in st st beg with a K row, as folls:

Row 1 (RS): Using yarn **B** K2 [2: 3: 3], work next 7 sts as row 1 of chart, using yarn **B** K2 [2: 3: 3].

Row 2: Using yarn **B** P2 [2: 3: 3], work next 7 sts as row 2 of chart, using yarn **B** P2 [2: 3: 3].
These 2 rows set the chart - work chart with edge sts in st st using yarn **B**.
Keeping chart correct as now set, work rem 8 rows of chart, ending with RS facing for next row.
Cut off yarn **A** and continue throughout using yarn **B**.

0-3 months only

Row 1 (RS): K1, skpo, K to last 3 sts, K2tog, K1. 9 sts.

Row 2: P1, P2tog, P to last 3 sts, P2tog tbl, P1. 7 sts.
Cut off yarn.

[3-6: 6-9: 9-12] months only

Row 1 (RS): K1, skpo, K to last 3 sts, K2tog, K1. [9: 11: 11] sts.

Row 2: Purl.
Rep the last 2 rows once more. [7: 9: 9] sts.
Cut off yarn.

All sizes

With RS facing, using US 5 (3.75 mm) needles, rejoin yarn **B** to inner edge of first 10 [11: 11: 12] sts, pick up and knit 8 [10: 12: 14] sts evenly along right side of instep, knit across 7 [7: 9: 9] sts of toe, pick up and knit 8 [10: 12: 14] sts evenly along left side of instep and Knit across rem 10 [11: 11: 12] sts. 43 [49: 55: 61] sts.
Work in g st for 5 rows, ending with RS facing for next row.

Shape sole

Row 1 (RS): K1, skpo, K14 [17: 20: 23], K2tog, K5, skpo, K14 [17: 20: 23], K2tog, K1. 39 [45: 51: 57] sts.

Row 2 and every foll alt row: Knit.

Row 3: K1, skpo, K13 [16: 19: 22], K2tog, K3, skpo, K13 [16: 19: 22], K2tog, K1. 35 [41: 47: 53] sts.

Row 5: K1, skpo, K12 [15: 18: 21], K2tog, K1, skpo, K12 [15: 18: 21], K2tog, K1. 31 [37: 43: 49] sts.

Row 7: K1, skpo, K11 [14: 17: 20], sl 1, K2tog, psso, K11 [14: 17: 20], K2tog, K1. 27 [33: 39: 45] sts.

Row 8: Knit.
BO.

RIGHT BOOTIE

Work as given for left bootie.

FINISHING

Join row ends and sole edge of each bootie using backstitch or mattress stitch if preferred. Work the other bootie to match. Cut the length of ribbon in half and thread through the first row of eyelets above instep. Trim to size if required and tie into a bow at left side for left bootie and right side for right bootie as shown.

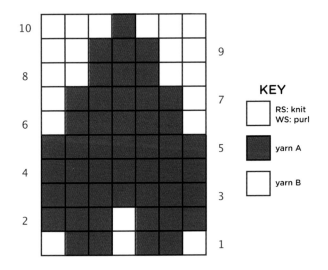

KEY

□ RS: knit
WS: purl

■ yarn A

□ yarn B

Rib With Cuff Booties

SIZES
0-6 [6-12] months

ABBREVIATIONS
See inside front flap

SPECIAL ABBREVIATION
P1 below purl into stitch 1 row below

MATERIALS NEEDED
🧶 **DMC Natura Just Cotton** (170 yd/155 m per 50g ball)
1 ball of Rose Layette (06)
🧶 US 2 (2.75 mm) needles
🧶 1yd (90 cm) of 5mm ribbon

GAUGE (TENSION)
29 sts and 38 rows to 4 in (10 cm) measured over st st using US 2 (2.75 mm) needles.

LEFT BOOTIE

Using US 2 (2.75 mm) needles CO 27 [31] sts.

Row 1 (RS): K1, (Kfb) twice, K8 [10], (Kfb) twice, K1, (Kfb) twice, K8 [10], (Kfb) twice, K1. 35 [39] sts.

Rows 2 and 4: Purl.

Row 3: K1, (Kfb) twice, K12 [14], (Kfb) twice, K1, (Kfb) twice, K12 [14], (Kfb) twice, K1. 43 [47] sts.

Row 5: K1, (Kfb) twice, K16 [18], (Kfb) twice, K1, (Kfb) twice, K16 [18], (Kfb) twice, K1. 51 [55] sts.
Beg with a P row, work 3 rows in st st. Mark each end of the first row with a colored thread and ending with RS facing for next row.

Picot row (RS): K1, *yo, K2tog, rep from * to end.
Beg with a P row st st 3 rows. Mark each end of last row with a colored thread and ending with RS facing for next row.

Row 1 (RS): K1, *K1 tbl, P1 below, rep from * to last 2 sts, K1 tbl, K1.

Row 2: K1, *P1 below, K1 tbl, rep from * to last 2 sts, P1 below, K1.
These 2 rows form patt.
Cont in patt for a further 12 [14] rows, ending with RS facing for next row.

Row 1 (RS): K21 [23], (K2tog) twice, K1, (K2tog) twice, K21 [23]. 47 [51] sts.

Row 2 and every foll alt row: Knit.

Row 3: K19 [21], (K2tog) twice, K1, (K2tog) twice, K19 [21]. 43 [47] sts.

Row 5: K17 [19], (K2tog) twice, K1, (K2tog) twice, K17 [19]. 39 [43] sts.

Row 6: Knit.
Beg with a K row, work in st st for 4 rows, ending with RS facing for next row.

Ribbon row (RS): K1 [3], *yo, K2tog, K3, rep from * to last 3 [0] sts, (yo, K2tog, K1) 1 [0] times.

Next row: Purl.

Divide for cuffs

Next row (RS): P16 [18], K3, slip these 19 [21] sts on a holder, BO next st (1 st on right needle), K2, P16 [18]. Working on these last 19 [21] sts only work as folls:

Row 1: Knit.

Row 2: K3, P to end.
Rep the last 2 rows 5 times more.

Working in st for 3 rows, ending with **WS** facing for next row. BO knitwise (on **WS**).

With RS of cuff facing, using US 2 (2.75 mm) needles, rejoin yarn to rem 19 [21] sts left on a holder and work as folls:

Row 1: Knit.

Row 2: P16 [18], K3.
Rep the last 2 rows 5 times more.
Working in st for 3 rows, ending with **WS** facing for next row. BO knitwise (on **WS**).

RIGHT BOOTIE

Work as given for left bootie.

FINISHING

Join row ends and sole edge of each bootie using backstitch or mattress stitch if preferred, reversing seam for cuff. With WS of work facing, fold work at picot row and slip stitch together the 2 rows marked with color threads all around bootie, thus forming a picot edge on RS. Cut the length of ribbon in half and thread through ribbon row. Trim to size if required and tie into a bow at front as shown.

Green and White Booties with Ankle Straps

SIZES
0-6 [6-12] months

ABBREVIATIONS
See inside front flap

MATERIALS NEEDED
- **DMC Natura Just Cotton** (170 yd/155 m per 50g ball)
1 ball of Ibiza (01) **A**
1 ball of Light Green (12) **B**
- US 2 (2.75 mm) needles
- 2 x 10 mm buttons

GAUGE (TENSION)
29 sts and 38 rows to 4 in (10 cm) measured over st st using US 2 (2.75 mm) needles.

LEFT BOOTIE

Using US 2 (2.75 mm) needles and yarn **A** CO 47 [49] sts.

Row 1 (RS): K1, *P1, K1, rep from * to end.

Row 2: P1, *K1, P1, rep from * to end.

Stripe patt

Row 1 (RS): Using yarn **B** Knit.

Row 2: Using yarn **B** P1, *K1, P1, rep from * to end.

Row 3: Using yarn **A** Knit.

Row 4: Using yarn **A** P1, *K1, P1, rep from * to end.
These 4 rows form patt.

Cont in patt for a further 18 [22] rows, ending with row 2 of stripe patt and RS facing for next row.
Cut off yarns.

Next row (RS): Slip first 17 sts on a holder, rejoin yarns **A** and **B** patt until there are 13 [15] sts on right needle and turn, leaving rem sts on a holder.
Keeping continuity of stripe pattern work a further 9 [13] rows on these 13 [15] sts only for instep and ending with RS facing for next row.

Cut off yarn **A** and cont using yarn **B** throughout.
Work in g st for 6 rows, ending with RS facing for next row.

Cut off yarn.

With RS facing, using US 2 (2.75 mm) needles and yarn **B**, rejoin and knit across first 17 sts from holder, pick up and knit 8 [11] sts evenly along right side of instep, knit across 13 [15] sts of toe, pick up and knit 8 [11] sts evenly along left side of instep and knit across rem 17 sts from holder. 63 [71] sts.

Next row (WS): Knit.

Shape toe

Row 1 (RS): K34 [38], turn.

Row 2: Sl 1, K4, turn.

Row 3: Sl 1, K5, turn.

Row 4: Sl 1, K6, turn.

Row 5: Sl 1, K7, turn.

Row 6: Sl 1, K8, turn.

Row 7: Sl 1, K9, turn.

Row 8: Sl 1, K10, turn.

Row 9: Sl 1, K to end of row.
Work in g st for 3 [5] rows, across all 63 [71] sts.
Work in g st for 2 rows, dec 1 st at each end of every row. 59 [67] sts.

Shape sole

Row 1 (RS): K35 [39], turn.

Row 2: Sl 1, K10, turn.

Row 3: Sl 1, K9, K2tog, turn.
Rep the last row until 31 sts rem (10 sts unworked at each side of sole).

Next row: Sl 1, K9, K3tog, turn.
Next row: Sl 1, K8, K3tog, turn.

Next row: Sl 1, K7, K3tog, turn.

Next row: Sl 1, K to end of row.
BO knitwise (on **WS**) for back edge of heel, marking centre st with a colored thread.

LEFT STRAP

Using US 2 (2.75 mm) needles and yarn **B** CO 44 [46] sts. Work 2 rows in g st, ending with RS facing for next row.

Buttonhole row (RS): K2, yo, K2tog, K to end.

Next row: Knit.
BO.

RIGHT BOOTIE

Work as given for left bootie.

RIGHT STRAP

Using US 2 (2.75 mm) needles and yarn **B** CO 44 [46] sts.

Work 2 rows in g st, ending with RS facing for next row.

Buttonhole row (RS): K to last 4 sts, K2tog, yo, K2.

Next row: Knit.
BO.

FINISHING

Join row ends of each bootie using backstitch or mattress stitch if preferred. Place colored thread to centre back seam and join across to form back edge of heel. Sew on button 2 sts from opposite end of buttonhole on each strap. Place around booties as illustrated then fasten button. If desired you can attach the middle of each ankle strap with a few stitches at the back of booties.

Picot Flower Booties

SIZES
0-3 [3-6: 6-9: 9-12] months

ABBREVIATIONS
See inside front flap

MATERIALS NEEDED
✄ **DMC Woolly** (136 yd/125 m per 50g ball)
1 ball of Pink (042) **A**
1 ball of White (001) **B**
✄ US 3 (3.25 mm) needles
✄ US 5 (3.75 mm) needles
✄ 2 x 15 mm buttons

GAUGE (TENSION)
25 sts and 34 rows to 4 in (10 cm) measured over st st using US 5 (3.75 mm) needles.

LEFT BOOTIE

Using US 3 (3.25 mm) needles and yarn **A** CO 31 [35: 39: 43] sts.
Beg with a K row, work in st st for 3 rows, ending with **WS** facing for next row.

Picot row (WS): K1, *yo, K2tog, rep from * to end.
Beg with a K row, work in st st for 3 rows, ending with **WS** facing for next row.
Break off yarn **A** and change to yarn **B**.

Joining row (WS): *Purl next st tog with corresponding CO st below st on needle, rep from * to end. (This completes the picot section).

Row 1 (RS): K1, *P1, K1, rep from * to end.

Row 2: P1, *K1, P1, rep from * to end.
These 2 rows form rib.
Cont in rib for a further 15 [17: 19: 21] rows, ending with **WS** facing for next row.

Change to US 5 (3.75 mm) needles.
Beg with a K row, work in st st for 4 [6: 6: 8] rows, ending with RS facing for next row.

Shape instep

Row 1 (RS): K20 [23: 26: 29], turn.

Row 2: P until there are 9 [11: 13: 15] sts on right needle and turn.
Working on these 9 [11: 13: 15] sts only work as folls:
Beg with a K row, work in st st for 14 [16: 18: 20] rows, ending with RS facing for next row.
Cut off yarn.

With RS facing, using US 5 (3.75 mm) needles and yarn **B**, rejoin to inner edge of first 11 [12: 13: 14] sts, pick up and knit 9 [10: 11: 12] sts evenly along right side of instep, knit across 9 [11: 13: 15] sts of toe, pick up and knit 9 [10: 11: 12] sts evenly along left side of instep and knit across rem 11 [12: 13: 14] sts. 49 [55: 61: 67] sts.
Beg with a P row, work in st st for 7 [9: 9: 11] rows, ending with RS facing for next row.
Cut off yarn **B** and change to yarn **A**.
Beg with a K row, work 4 rows in st st, ending with RS facing for next row.

Picot row (RS): K1, *yo, K2tog, rep from * to end.
Beg with a P row, work 3 rows in st st 3 rows, ending with RS facing for next row.
Cut off yarn **A** and change to yarn **B**.

Joining row (RS): *Knit next st tog with corresponding st 8 rows below st on needle, rep from * to end. (This completes the picot section).

Shape sole

Rows 1 and 3: Knit.

Row 2: K1, skpo, K18 [21: 24: 27], K2tog, K3, skpo, K18 [21: 24: 27], K2tog, K1. 45 [51: 57: 63] sts.

Row 4: K1, skpo, K16 [19: 22: 25], K2tog, K3, skpo, K16 [19: 22: 25], K2tog, K1. 41 [47: 53: 59] sts.

Row 5: K1, skpo, K14 [17: 20: 23], K2tog, K3, skpo, K14 [17: 20: 23], K2tog, K1. 37 [43: 49: 55] sts.

[3-6: 6-9: 9-12] months only
Next row: K1, skpo, K- [15: 18: 21], K2tog, K3, skpo, K- [15: 18: 21], K2tog, K1. - [39: 45: 51] sts.

[6-9: 9-12] months only

Next row: K1, skpo, K- [-: 16: 19], K2tog, K3, skpo, K- [-: 16: 19], K2tog, K1. - [-: 41: 47] sts.

[9-12] months only
Next row: K1, skpo, K- [-: -: 17], K2tog, K3, K2tog, K- [-: -: 17], K2tog, K1. - [-: -: 43] sts.

All sizes

Next row: Knit.
BO.

RIGHT BOOTIE

Work as given for left bootie.

FINISHING
Join row ends and sole edge of each bootie using backstitch or mattress stitch if preferred, reversing seam for cuff.

FLOWERS (make 2)

Using US 3 (3.25 mm) needles and yarn **A** CO 2 sts.

Row 1 (RS): Kfb, K1. 3 sts.

Rows 2, and 4: Knit.

Row 3: Kfb, K2. 4 sts.

Row 5: Kfb, K3. 5 sts.

Row 6: Knit.

Row 7: BO 3 sts (1 st on right needle), K1. 2 sts.

Row 8: Knit.

These 8 rows for patt.
Cont in patt for a further 30 rows, ending with row 6 of patt and RS facing for next row. 5 sts.
BO.

FINISHING
Join the 2 CO sts with the BO edge, taking care not to twist the petals. Run a gathering thread along the straight edge, pull up tightly and fasten off securely. Sew a button onto each flower centre then attach to top of each bootie as shown.

Flower Shoes

SIZES
0-6 [6-12] months

ABBREVIATIONS
See inside front flap

MATERIALS NEEDED
🧶 **DMC Natura Just Cotton** (170 yd/155 m per 50g ball)
1 ball of Nacar (35) **A**
1 ball of Crimson (61) **B**
1 ball of Chartreuse (48) **C**
🧶 US 2 (2.75 mm) needles
🧶 2 x 12 [15] mm buttons

GAUGE (TENSION)
29 sts and 38 rows to 4 in (10 cm) measured over st st using US 2 (2.75 mm) needles.

SHOES

UPPERS (make 2)

Using US 2 (2.75 mm) needles and yarn **A** CO 8 [10] sts for toe edge.

Next row (WS): Purl.

Next row: K1, *M1, K1, rep from * to end. 15 [19] sts.
Beg with a P row, work in st st throughout, inc 1 st at each end of next 4 rows then 2 foll alt rows, ending with **WS** facing for next row. 27 [31] sts.
Beg with a P row, work in st st for 7 [11] rows, ending with RS facing for next row.

Divide for sides

First Side

Next row (RS): Knit until there are 12 [13] sts on right needle and turn.
Working on these 12 [13] sts only work as folls:

Next row (WS): P1, P2tog, P to end. 11 [12] sts.

Next row: Knit.

Next row: P1, P2tog, P to end. 10 [11] sts.
Beg with a K row, work in st st for 3 rows, ending with **WS** facing for next row.

Next row (WS): P1, P2tog, P to end. 9 [10] sts.
Beg with a K row, work in st st for 16 [20] rows, ending with RS facing for next row, placing a marker at end of 12th [16th] row.
BO for centre.

Second side

With RS facing, slip centre 3 [5] sts on a holder.
Using US 2 (2.75 mm) needles rejoin yarn A to rem 12 [13] sts and K to end. 12 [13] sts.

Next row (WS): P to last 3 sts, P2tog tbl, P1. 11 [12] sts.

Next row: Knit.

Next row: P to last 3 sts, P2tog tbl, P1. 10 [11] sts.
Beg with a K row, work in st st for 3 rows, ending with **WS** facing for next row.

Next row (WS): P to last 3 sts, P2tog tbl, P1. 9 [10] sts.
Beg with a K row, work in st st for 16 [20] rows, ending with RS facing for next row, placing a marker at beg of 12th [16th] row.
BO for centre back.

EDGING

With RS facing, using US 2 (2.75 mm) needles and yarn **B**, starting at inner BO edge of first side, pick up and knit 17 [19] sts evenly along left side to centre 3 [5] sts on a holder, knit across 3 [5] sts from holder, pick up and knit 17 [19] sts up right side to inner BO edge of second side. 37 [43] sts.
BO knitwise (on **WS**).
Work other shoe to match.

SOLES (make 2)

Using US 2 (2.75 mm) needles and yarn **A** CO 7 [9] sts for toe edge.

Next row (WS): Purl.
Beg with a K row, work in st st throughout, inc 1 st at each end of next 3 rows then 2 foll alt rows, ending with **WS** facing for next row. 17 [19] sts.
Beg with a P row, work in st st for 7 [9] rows, ending with RS facing for next row.

Next row (RS): K1, skpo, K to last 3 sts, K2tog, K1. 15 [17] sts.

Rep the last 8 [10] rows twice more. 11 [13] sts.
Beg with a P row, work in st st for 7 [9] rows, ending with RS facing for next row.
BO for back edge.

STRAPS (make 2)

Using US 2 (2.75 mm) needles and yarn **B** CO 27 [33] sts.
BO knitwise.

ROSES (make 2)

Using US 2 (2.75 mm) needles and yarn **B** CO 29 [33] sts.
Beg with a K row, work in st st for 3 rows, ending with **WS** facing for next row.

Row 4 (WS): K1, *yo, K2tog, rep from * to end.
Beg with a K row, work in st st for 3 rows, ending with **WS** facing for next row.
BO purlwise (on **WS**).

LEAVES (make 4)

Using US 2 (2.75 mm) needles and yarn **C** CO 11 [15] sts.

Rows 1 and 2: K9 [12], turn and K to end.

Rows 3 and 4: K7 [10], turn and K to end.

Rows 5 and 6: K5 [8], turn and K to end.

Rows 7 and 8: K3 [4], turn and K to end.

Row 9: Knit across all sts.
BO knitwise (on **WS**).

FINISHING

Placing CO edge of sole in line with markers on uppers and BO edge of uppers, sew in soles. Join CO edges of uppers and ends of edging, then sew lower row ends to CO sts of sole. Fold each strap in half, crossing ends and sew through both thicknesses to WS at inside edge of each shoe using photograph as a guide. Sew on button to outer edge of each shoe as shown.
Fold each rose piece in half so that CO and BO edges meet and oversew edges together. Tightly roll up doubled strip to form rose shape as in photograph and sew through base to secure. Using photograph as a guide, sew a rose onto each shoe upper.
Gather longer set of row ends and fasten off securely. Using photograph as a guide sew a leaf either side of each rose as shown.

Teddy Booties

SIZES

0-3 [3-6: 6-9: 9-12] months

ABBREVIATIONS

See inside front flap

MATERIALS NEEDED

🦊 **DMC Woolly** (136 yd/125 m per 50g ball)
1 ball of Light Brown (110) **A**
1 ball of Dark Brown (116) **B**
🦊 US 3 (3.25 mm) needles
🦊 US 5 (3.75 mm) needles

GAUGE (TENSION)

25 sts and 34 rows to 4 in (10 cm) measured over st st using US 5 (3.75 mm) needles.

LEFT BOOTIE

Using US 3 (3.25 mm) needles and yarn **A** CO 31 [35: 39: 43] sts.

Rows 1 (RS): K1, *P1, K1, rep from * to end.

Row 2: P1, *K1, P1, rep from * to end.
These 2 rows form rib.
Cont in rib for a further 19 [19: 21: 23] rows, ending with **WS** facing for next row.

Change to US 5 (3.75 mm) needles.
Beg with a K row, work in st st for 4 [4: 6: 8] rows, ending with RS facing for next row.

Shape instep

Row 1 (RS): K20 [23: 26: 29], turn.

Row 2: P until there are 9 [11: 13: 15] sts on right needle and turn.
Working on these 9 [11: 13: 15] sts only work as folls:
Beg with a K row, work in st st for 14 [16: 18: 20] rows, ending with RS facing for next row.
Cut off yarn.

With RS facing, using US 5 (3.75 mm) needles and yarn **A**, rejoin to inner edge of first 11 [12: 13: 14] sts, pick up and knit 9 [10: 11: 12] sts evenly along right side of instep, knit across 9 [11: 13: 15] sts of toe, pick up and

knit 9 [10: 11: 12] sts evenly along left side of instep and Knit across rem 11 [12: 13: 14] sts. 49 [55: 61: 67] sts.
Beg with a P row, work in st st for 9 [9: 11: 13] rows, ending with RS facing for next row.
Cut off yarn.

Shape sole

Change to yarn **B**.
Work in g st for 2 rows.

Row 1 (RS): K1, skpo, K18 [21: 24: 27], K2tog, K3, skpo, K18 [21: 24: 27], K2tog, K1. 45 [51: 57: 63] sts.

Row 2: Knit.

Row 3: K1, skpo, K16 [19: 22: 25], K2tog, K3, skpo, K16 [19: 22: 25], K2tog, K1. 41 [47: 53: 59] sts.

Row 4: K1, skpo, K14 [17: 20: 23], K2tog, K3, skpo, K14 [17: 20: 23], K2tog, K1. 37 [43: 49: 55] sts.

[3-6: 6-9: 9-12] months only
Next row: K1, skpo, K— [15: 18: 21], K2tog, K3, skpo, K— [15: 18: 21], K2tog, K1. — [39: 45: 51] sts.

[6-9: 9-12] months only
Next row: K1, skpo, K— [—: 16: 19], K2tog, K3, skpo, K— [—: 16: 19], K2tog, K1. — [—: 41: 47] sts.

[9-12] months only
Next row: K1, skpo, K— [—: —: 17], K2tog, K3, skpo, K— [—: —: 17], K2tog, K1. — [—: —: 43] sts.

For all sizes

Next row: Knit.
BO.

RIGHT BOOTIE

Work as given for left bootie.

EARS

OUTERS (make 4)

Using US 3 (3.25 mm) needles and yarn **B** CO 10 sts for lower edge.
Beg with a K row, work in st st for 5 rows, ending with **WS** facing for next row.
Dec 1 st at each end of next 3 rows, ending with RS facing for next row. 4 sts.
BO for top edge.

INNERS (make 4)

Work as given for outers using yarn **A** throughout.

FINISHING
Join row ends and sole edge of each bootie using backstitch or mattress stitch if preferred, reversing seam for cuff.
Taking an inner and outer ear piece join ears in pairs matching CO and BO edges together, slightly curving ear pin CO edge to top of instep as shown. Sew as pinned. Work the other ear in the same manner on the opposite side of instep.
Using yarn **B** work facial features by working straight stitches as shown on front of instep. Work the other bootie to match.

Bumble Bee Shoes

SIZES
0-6 [6-12] months

ABBREVIATIONS
See inside front flap

MATERIALS NEEDED
🧶 **DMC Natura Just Cotton** (170 yd/155 m per 50g ball)
1 ball of Noir (11) **A**
1 ball of Golden Lemon (43) **B**
1 ball of Crimson (61) **C**
🧶 US 2 (2.75 mm) needles

GAUGE (TENSION)
29 sts and 38 rows to 4 in (10 cm) measured over st st using US 2 (2.75 mm) needles.

STRIPE SEQUENCE
Rows 1 to 4: Using yarn **B**.
Rows 5 to 8: Using yarn **A**.
These 8 rows form stripes

SHOES

UPPERS (make 2)
Using US 2 (2.75 mm) needles and yarn **A** CO 8 [10] sts for toe edge.

Next row (WS): Purl.
Beg with stripe row 1 and a K row, now work in st st in stripe sequence (see above) throughout as folls:

Next row (RS): K1, *M1, K1, rep from * to end. 15 [19] sts.
Keeping stripes correct, inc 1 st at each end of next 4 rows then 2 foll alt rows, ending with **WS** facing for next row. 27 [31] sts.
Work 7 [11] rows, ending with RS facing for next row.

Divide for sides

First Side
Keeping stripes correct work as folls:

Next row (RS): Patt until there are 12 [13] sts on right needle and turn.
Working on these 12 [13] sts only work as folls:

Next row (WS): P1, P2tog, P to end. 11 [12] sts.
Work 1 row.

Next row: P1, P2tog, P to end. 10 [11] sts.
Work 3 rows, ending with **WS** facing for next row.

Next row (WS): P1, P2tog, P to end. 9 [10] sts.
Work 16 [20] rows, ending with RS facing for next row,

placing a marker at end of 12th [16th] row.
BO for centre.

Second side

Keeping stripes correct work as folls:
With RS facing, slip centre 3 [5] sts on a holder.
Using US 2 (2.75 mm) needles rejoin appropriate yarn to rem 12 [13] sts and K to end. 12 [13] sts.

Next row (WS): P to last 3 sts, P2tog tbl, P1. 11 [12] sts.
Work 1 row.

Next row: P to last 3 sts, P2tog tbl, P1. 10 [11] sts.
Work 3 rows, ending with **WS** facing for next row.

Next row (WS): P to last 3 sts, P2tog tbl, P1. 9 [10] sts.
Work 16 [20] rows, ending with RS facing for next row, placing a marker at beg of 12th [16th] row.
BO for centre back.

EDGING

With RS facing, using US 2 (2.75 mm) needles and yarn **A**, starting at inner BO edge of first side, pick up and knit 17 [19] sts evenly along left side to centre 3 [5] sts on a holder, knit across 3 [5] sts from holder, pick up and knit 17 [19] sts up right side to inner BO edge of second side. 37 [43] sts.
BO knitwise (on **WS**).
Work other shoe to match.

SOLES (make 2)

Using US 2 (2.75 mm) needles and yarn **A** CO 7 [9] sts for toe edge.

Next row (WS): Purl.

Beg with a K row, work in st st throughout, inc 1 st at each end of next 3 rows then 2 foll alt rows, ending with **WS** facing for next row. 17 [19] sts.
Beg with a P row, work in st st for 7 [9] rows, ending with RS facing for next row.

Next row (RS): K1, skpo, K to last 3 sts, K2tog, K1. 15 [17] sts.

Rep the last 8 [10] rows twice more. 11 [13] sts.

Beg with a P row, work in st st for 7 [9] rows, ending with RS facing for next row.
BO for back edge.

STRAPS (make 2)

Using US 2 (2.75 mm) needles and yarn **A** CO 31 [37] sts.
BO knitwise.

FLOWERS (make 2)

Using US 2 (2.75 mm) needles and yarn **C** CO 7 sts.

Row 1 (WS): Purl.

Row 2: Kfb into every st. 14 sts.

Row 3: Purl.

Row 4: K4, yo, *K2, yo, rep from * to last 4 sts, K4. 18 sts.

Row 5: Purl.

Row 6: (K2tog) twice, K1, (K2tog, K1) 3 times, (K2tog) twice. 11 sts.

Beg with a P row, work in st st for 2 rows, ending with **WS** facing for next row.

Row 9 (WS): P1, (P2tog) 5 times. 6 sts.
Cut off yarn, thread through rems sts, pull up tightly and fasten off securely.

FINISHING

Placing CO edge of sole in line with markers on uppers and BO edge of uppers, sew in soles. Join CO edges of uppers and ends of edging, then sew lower row ends to CO sts of sole. Fold each strap in half, crossing ends and sew through both thicknesses to WS at inside edge of each shoe using photograph as a guide.

Take each flower and gather up the CO sts tightly and fasten off. With RS outside catch the two sets of row ends together, but leave the petal tips row ends separated. Secure a length of yarn **B** at underside of flower centre. Pass needle and yarn through to gathered CO sts and work a few stitches to form a small dot. Fasten off underneath flower. Sew a flower to opposite outer edge of strap of each shoe as shown.

Daisy Sandals

SIZES
0-3 [3-6: 6-9: 9-12] months

ABBREVIATIONS
See inside front flap

MATERIALS NEEDED
✿ **DMC Natura Just Cotton** (170 yd/155 m per 50g ball)
1 ball of Ibiza (01) **A**
1 ball of Bamboo (76) **B**
1 ball of Tournesol (16) **C**
✿ US 2 (2.75 mm) needles
✿ US 2 (2.75 mm) circular needle

GAUGE (TENSION)
27 sts and 54 rows to 4 in (10 cm) measured over g st using US 2 (2.75 mm) needles.

SANDALS

SOLES (make 2)

Using US 2 (2.75 mm) needles and yarn **A** CO 6 sts for heel edge.

Row 1 (RS): Sl 1, K4, P1.

Row 2: Sl 1, K1, yo, K2, yo, K1, P1. 8 sts.

Row 3: Sl 1, K1, K1 tbl, K2, K1 tbl, K1, P1.

Row 4: Sl 1, K1, yo, K4, yo, K1, P1. 10 sts.

Row 5: Sl 1, K1, K1 tbl, K4, K1 tbl, K1, P1.

Row 6: Sl 1, K1, yo, K6, yo, K1, P1. 12 sts.

Row 7: Sl 1, K1, K1 tbl, K6, K1 tbl, K1, P1.

Next row: Sl 1, K10, P1.
Rep the last row 11 [13: 15: 19] times more, ending with

WS facing for next row.

Next row (WS): Sl 1, K1, yo, K8, yo, K1, P1. 14 sts.

Next row: Sl 1, K1, K1 tbl, K8, K1 tbl, K1, P1.

Next row: Sl 1, K1, yo, K10, yo, K1, P1. 16 sts.

Next row: Sl 1, K1, K1 tbl, K10, K1 tbl, K1, P1.

Next row: Sl 1, K14, P1.

Rep the last row 11 [13: 15: 19] times more, ending with

WS facing for next row.
Place a colour marker at each end of last row.

Next row (WS): Sl 1, K1, skpo, K8, K2tog, K1, P1. 14 sts.

Next row: Sl 1, K12, P1.

Next row: Sl 1, K1, skpo, K6, K2tog, K1, P1. 12 sts.

Next row: Sl 1, K10, P1.

Next row: Sl 1, K1, skpo, K4, K2tog, K1, P1. 10 sts.

Next row: Sl 1, K8, P1.
BO knitwise (on **WS**) for front edge.

SIDE EDGES (both alike)

With RS facing using US 2 (2.75 mm) circular needle and yarn **B** pick up and knit 17 [19: 21: 23] sts evenly down left side of sole from marker to CO edge of heel, pick up and knit 5 sts evenly along CO edge of heel, then pick up and knit 17 [19: 21: 23] sts evenly along right side of sole to marker. 39 [43: 47: 51] sts.

Working backwards and forwards in rows, not rounds, work as folls:

Next row (WS): K1, *P1, K1, rep from * to end.

Last row forms seed (moss) st.
Work a further 11 [13: 15: 17] rows in seed (moss) st, ending with **WS** facing for next row.

BO knitwise (on **WS**).

DAISIES (make 2)

Using US 2 (2.75 mm) needles and yarn **A** CO 13 sts.
Beg with a P, work 2 rows in st st, ending with **WS** facing for next row.

Picot row (WS): K1, (yo, K1) to end. 25 sts.

Next row: Knit.

Next row: P1, (P2tog) to end. 13 sts.
BO.

CENTRE PIECE (make 2)

Using US 2 (2.75 mm) needles and yarn **C** CO 9 sts.
Cut off yarn leaving an end, thread through sts, pull up tightly and fasten off securely.

FINISHING

With RS outside, oversew CO and BO edges of each daisy together. Catch the two sets of row ends together, leaving the petal tips (picot row) row ends separated. There will be a hole at centre of the daisies which will be covered by the centre pieces. Sew a centre piece to CO edge of each daisy. Join first and last BO st together of side edge on each sandal to form top of foot, then sew a daisy to front where you have just joined using photograph as a guide. Using yarn **B** work a line of small chain stitches around front edge on sole using as shown in photograph.

Double Crossover Shoes

SIZES
0-6 [6-12] months

ABBREVIATIONS
See inside front flap

MATERIALS NEEDED
🦎 **DMC Natura Just Cotton** (170 yd/155 m per 50g ball)
1 ball of Prusian (64) **A**
1 ball of Aquamarina (25) **B**
🦎 US 2 (2.75 mm) needles
🦎 4 x 10 mm buttons

GAUGE (TENSION)
27 sts and 54 rows to 4 in (10 cm) measured over g st using US 2 (2.75 mm) needles.

LEFT SHOE

Using US 2 (2.75 mm) needles and yarn **A** CO 33 [37] sts.

Row 1 (RS): Knit.

Row 2: K1, yo, K15 [17], yo, K1, yo, K15 [17], yo, K1. 37 [41] sts.

Rows 3, 5, 7 and 9: Knit, working K1 tbl into every yo of previous row.

Row 4: K1, yo, K16 [18], yo, K3, yo, K16 [18], yo, K1. 41 [45] sts.

Row 6: K1, yo, K17 [19], yo, K5, yo, K17 [19], yo, K1. 45 [49] sts.

Row 8: K1, yo, K18 [20], yo, K7, yo, K18 [20], yo, K1. 49 [53] sts.

Row 10: K1, yo, K19 [21], yo, K9, yo, K19 [21], yo, K1. 53 [57] sts.

Row 11: As row 3.
Work in g st for 3 [5] rows, ending with RS facing for next row.

Cut off yarn **A** and change to yarn **B**.
Work in g st for 1 row, ending with **WS** facing for next row.

Next row: K1, *P1, K1, rep from * to end.
Last row forms seed (moss) st.

Cont in seed (moss) st for a further 3 [5] rows, ending with **WS** facing for next row.

Shape shoe

Next row (WS): K1, (P1, K1) 9 [10] times, P3tog, (K3tog, P3tog) twice, K1, (P1, K1) 9 [10] times. 43 [47] sts.

Next row (RS): K1, *P1, K1, rep from * to end.
Last row forms seed (moss) st.
Cont in seed (moss) st for a further 2 rows, ending with **WS** facing for next row.

Divide for straps

Next row (WS): (K1, P1) 5 [6] times, BO next 23 sts (1 st on right needle), patt to end.

First strap

Working on first set of 10 [12] sts only, work as folls:
Patt 1 row, turn and CO 15 [17] sts. 25 [29] sts.

Next row (WS): K1, *P1, K1, rep from * to end.
Rep last row once more, ending with **WS** facing for next row.

Next row (buttonhole row) (WS): P2tog, yo (to make a buttonhole), patt to end.
Patt 1 row.
BO in patt (on **WS**).

Second strap

With RS facing, using US 2 (2.75 mm) needles rejoin yarn **B** to inner edge of rem 10 [12] sts and CO 15 [17] sts, then work across as folls: K1, *P1, K1, rep from * to end. 25 [29] sts.

Next row (WS): K1, *P1, K1, rep from * to end.

Next row (buttonhole row) (RS): P2tog, yo (to make a buttonhole), patt to end.
Patt 1 row.
BO in patt.

RIGHT SHOE

Work as given for left shoe.

FINISHING

Join row ends and sole edge of each shoe using backstitch or mattress stitch if preferred. Sew on buttons.

Mary Jane Leaf Shoes

SIZES
0-3 [3-6: 6-9: 9-12] months

ABBREVIATIONS
See inside front flap

MATERIALS NEEDED
✄ **DMC Natura Just Cotton** (170 yd/155 m per 50g ball)
1 ball of Blé (83)
✄ US 2 (2.75 mm) needles
✄ 2 x 10 mm buttons

GAUGE (TENSION)
27 sts and 54 rows to 4 in (10 cm) measured over g st using US 2 (2.75 mm) needles.

LEFT SHOE

*Using US 2 (2.75 mm) needles CO 35 [41: 47: 53] sts.

Row 1 (RS): Knit.

Row 2: K1, yo, K16 [19: 22: 25], yo, K1, yo, K16 [19: 22: 25], yo, K1. 39 [45: 51: 57] sts.

Rows 3, 5 and 7: Knit, working K1 tbl into every yo of previous row.

Row 4: K2, yo, K16 [19: 22: 25], yo, K3, yo, K16 [19: 22: 25], yo, K2. 43 [49: 55: 61] sts.

Row 6: K3, yo, K16 [19: 22: 25], yo, K5, yo, K16 [19: 22: 25], yo, K3. 47 [53: 59: 65] sts.

Row 8: K4, yo, K16 [19: 22: 25], yo, K7, yo, K16 [19: 22: 25], yo, K4. 51 [57: 63: 69] sts.

Row 9: Knit, working K1 tbl into every yo of previous row. Work in g st for 5 [7: 7: 9] rows, ending with RS facing for next row.

Shape instep

Next row (RS): K21 [24: 26: 29], P9 [9: 11: 11] skpo, turn.

Next row: P1, K9 [9: 11: 11], P2tog, turn.

0-3 months only

Row 1 (RS): K1, P4, yo, K1, yo, P4, skpo, turn.

Row 2: P1, K4, P3, K4, P2tog, turn.

Row 3: K1, P4, K1, (yo, K1) twice, P4, skpo, turn.

Row 4: P1, K4, P5, K4, P2tog, turn.

Row 5: K1, P4, K2, yo, K1, yo, K2, P4, skpo, turn.

Row 6: P1, K4, P7, K4, P2tog, turn.

Row 7: K1, P4, skpo, K3, K2tog, P4, skpo, turn.

Row 8: As row 4.

Row 9: K1, P4, skpo, K1, K2tog, P4, skpo, turn.

Row 10: As row 2.

Row 11: K1, P4, Sl 1, K2tog, psso, P4, skpo, turn.

Row 12: P1, K9, P2tog, turn.

[3-6] months only

Row 1 (RS): K1, P9, skpo, turn.

Row 2: P1, K9, P2tog, turn.

Rows 3 to 14: Work rows 1 to 12 as given for 0-3 months only.

Row 15: K1, P9, skpo, turn.

Row 16: P1, K9, skpo, turn.

[6-9] months only

Row 1 (RS): K1, P5, yo, K1, yo, P5, skpo, turn.

Row 2: P1, K5, P3, K5, P2tog, turn.

Row 3: K1, P5, K1, (yo, K1) twice, P5, skpo, turn.

Row 4: P1, K5, P5, K5, P2tog, turn.

Row 5: K1, P5, K2, yo, K1, yo, K2, P5, skpo, turn.

Row 6: P1, K5, P7, K5, P2tog, turn.

Row 7: K1, P5, K3, yo, K1, yo, K3, P5, skpo, turn.

Row 8: P1, K5, P9, K5, P2tog, turn.

Row 9: K1, P5, skpo, K5, K2tog, P5, skpo, turn.

Row 10: P1, K5, P7, K5, P2tog, turn.

Row 11: K1, P5, skpo, K3, K2tog, P5, skpo.

Row 12: P1, K5, P5, K5, P2tog, turn.

Row 13: K1, P5, skpo, K1, K2tog, P5, skpo, turn.

Row 14: P1, K5, P3, K5, P2tog, turn.

Row 15: K1, P5, sl 1, K2tog, psso, P5, skpo, turn.

Row 16: P1, K11, P2tog, turn.

[9-12] months only

Row 1 (RS): K1, P11, skpo, turn.

Row 2: P1, K11, P2tog, turn.

Rows 3 to 18: Work rows 1 to 16 as given for [9-12] months only.

Row 19: K1, P11, skpo, turn.

Row 20: P1, K11, P2tog, turn.

All sizes

Next row (RS): K10 [10: 12: 12], skpo, turn.

Next row: P1, K9 [9: 11: 11], P2tog, K to end. 37 [39: 43: 47] sts.
Work in g st for 1 row, ending with **WS** facing for next row.
BO knitwise (on **WS**). **

LEFT STRAP

Join row ends and sole edge of shoe using backstitch or mattress stitch if preferred.
With RS facing, using US 2 (2.75 mm) needles, pick up and knit 8 sts either side of centre back seam evenly. 16 sts.

Row 1 (WS): CO 3 sts (for button tab), K to end, turn and CO 15 [19: 23: 27] sts (for strap). 34 [38: 42: 46] sts.

Row 2: Knit.

Row 3 (buttonhole row) (WS): K to last 5 sts, K2tog, yo (to make a buttonhole), K3.

Row 4: Knit.

BO knitwise (on **WS**).

RIGHT SHOE

Work as given for left shoe from * to **.

RIGHT STRAP

Join row ends and sole edge of shoe using backstitch or mattress stitch if preferred.

With RS facing, using US 2 (2.75 mm) needles, pick up and knit 8 sts either side of centre back seam evenly. 16 sts.

Row 1 (WS): CO 15 [19: 23: 27] sts (for strap), K to end, turn and CO 3 sts (for button tab). 34 [38: 42: 46] sts.

Row 2: Knit.

Row 3 (buttonhole row) (WS): K3, yo, K2tog (to make a buttonhole), K to end.

Row 4: Knit.
BO knitwise (on **WS**).

FINISHING

Sew on buttons to correspond with buttonholes.

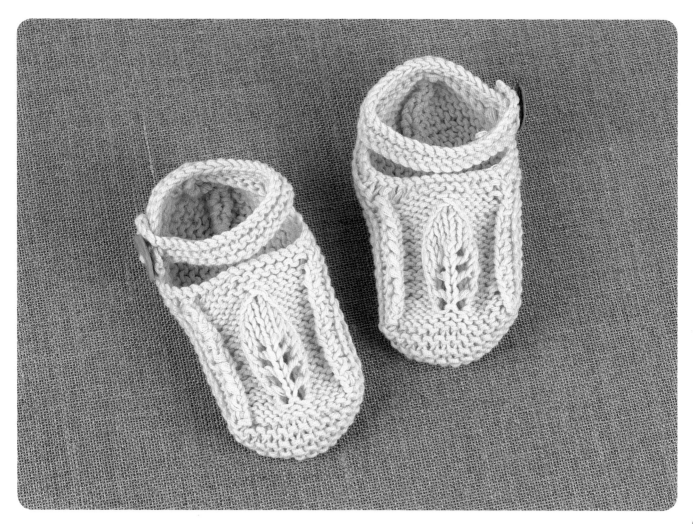

Sneakers

SIZES
0-6 [6-12] months

ABBREVIATIONS
See inside front flap

MATERIALS NEEDED
🧶 **DMC Natura Just Cotton** (170 yd/155 m per 50g ball)
1 ball of Star Light (27) **A**
1 ball of Brique (86) **B**
1 ball of Ibiza (01) **C**
🧶 US 2 (2.75 mm) needles

GAUGE (TENSION)
29 sts and 38 rows to 4 in (10 cm) measured over st st
using US 2 (2.75 mm) needles.

LEFT SNEAKER

LEFT SIDE

Using US 2 (2.75 mm) needles and yarn **A** CO 15 sts.
Work in g st for 4 rows, ending with RS facing for next row.

Next row (RS): Kfb, K to end. 16 sts.

Next row (shoe lace hole row) (WS): P to last 3 sts, yo,
P2tog (to make a lace hole), K1.

Next row: Kfb, K to end. 17 sts.

Next row: P to last st, K1.

Next row: Kfb, K to end. 18 sts.
Rep the last 2 rows 1 [2] times more. 19 [20] sts.

Next row (shoe lace hole row) (WS): P to last 3 sts, yo,
P2tog (to make a lace hole), K1.

Next row: Kfb, K to end. 20 [21] sts.

Next row: P to last st, K1.

Next row: Kfb, K to end. 21 [22] sts.
Rep the last 2 rows 1 [2] times more. 22 [24] sts.

Next row (shoe lace hole row) (WS): P to last 3 sts, yo,
P2tog (to make a lace hole), K1.

Next row: Kfb, K to end. 23 [25] sts.

Next row: P to last st, K1.
Cut off yarn and leave these 23 [25] sts on a holder.

FRONT TAB

Using US 2 (2.75 mm) needles and yarn **B** CO 14 [16] sts.
Work in g st for 2 rows, ending with RS facing for next row.
Beg with a K row, work in st st for 20 [24] rows.
Cut off yarn and leave these 14 [16] sts on a second holder.

RIGHT SIDE

Using US 2 (2.75 mm) needles and yarn **A** CO 15 sts.
Work in g st for 4 rows, ending with RS facing for next row.

Next row (RS): K to last 2 sts, Kfb, K1. 16 sts.

Next row (shoe lace hole row) (WS): K1, P2tog, yo (to make a lace hole), P to end.

Next row: K to last 2 sts, Kfb, K1. 17 sts.

Next row: K1, P to end.

Next row: K to last 2 sts, Kfb, K1. 18 sts.
Rep the last 2 rows 1 [2] times more. 19 [20] sts.

Next row (shoe lace hole row) (WS): K1, P2tog, yo (to make a lace hole), P to end.

Next row: K to last 2 sts, Kfb, K1. 20 [21] sts.

Next row: K1, P to end.

Next row: K to last 2 sts, Kfb, K1. 21 [22] sts.
Rep the last 2 rows 1 [2] times more. 22 [24] sts.

Next row (shoe lace hole row) (WS): K1, P2tog, yo (to make a lace hole), P to end.

Next row: K to last 2 sts, Kfb, K1. 23 [25] sts.

Next row: K1, P to end.

FOOT

Join sections
Next row (RS): Using yarn **A** knit all 23 [25] sts on needle, with RS facing knit across all 14 [16] sts of Front Tab left on second holder, then with RS facing knit across all 23 [25] sts of Left Side. 60 [66] sts.
Working in g st throughout, work as folls:
Work 1 [3] rows, ending with RS facing for next row.
Change to yarn **B**.

Work 2 rows, ending with RS facing for next row.
Cut off yarn **B** and change to yarn **A**.
Work 6 [8] rows, ending with RS facing for next row.
Cut off yarn **A** and cont in yarn **C** throughout as folls:
Work 4 [6] rows, ending with RS facing for next row.

Shape sole

Row 1 (RS): K5 [6], skpo, K16 [17], K2tog, K10 [12], skpo, K16 [17], K2tog, K5 [6]. 56 [62] sts.

Row 2 and every foll alt row: Knit.

Row 3: K4 [5], skpo, K16 [17], K2tog, K8 [10], skpo, K16 [17], K2tog, K4 [5]. 52 [58] sts.

Row 5: K3 [4], skpo, K16 [17], K2tog, K6 [8], skpo, K16 [17], K2tog, K3 [4]. 48 [54] sts.

Row 7: K2 [3], skpo, K16 [17], K2tog, K4 [6], skpo, K16 [17], K2tog, K2 [3]. 44 [50] sts.

Row 9: K1 [2], skpo, K16 [17], K2tog, K2 [4], skpo, K16 [17], K2tog, K1 [2]. 40 [46] sts.

Row 10: Knit.

For [6-12] months only

Next row (RS): K- [1], skpo, K- [17], K2tog, K- [2], skpo, K- [17], K2tog, K- [1]. - [42] sts.

Next row: Knit.

All sizes

Work in g st for 1 row, ending with **WS** facing for next row.
BO knitwise (on **WS**).

RIGHT SNEAKER

Work as given for left sneaker.

LACES (make 2)

Using US 2 (2.75 mm) needles and yarn **C** CO 156 [170] sts.
BO.

FINISHING

Join row ends and sole edge of each bootie using backstitch or mattress stitch if preferred. Thread laces as shown in photograph.

Double Strap Booties

SIZES

0-3 [3-6: 6-9: 9-12] months

ABBREVIATIONS

See inside front flap

MATERIALS NEEDED

🧶 **DMC Woolly** (136 yd/125 m per 50g ball)
1 ball of Beige (110) **A**
1 ball of Cream (003) **B**
🧶 US 3 (3.25 mm) needles
🧶 4 x 15 mm buttons

GAUGE (TENSION)

28 sts and 36 rows to 4 in (10 cm) measured over st st using US 3 (3.25 mm) needles.

LEFT BOOTIE

* Using US 3 (3.25 mm) needles and yarn **A** CO 19 [23: 27: 31] sts.

Row 1 (RS): Kfb into every st. 38 [46: 54: 62] sts.
Work in g st for 5 [5: 7: 7] rows, ending with RS facing for next row.
Cut off yarn **A** and join in yarn **B**.
Beg with a K row, work 6 rows in st st, ending with RS facing for next row.

Shape foot

[9-12] months only

Next row (RS): K26, K2tog, K6, skpo, K26. 60 sts.

Next row: P25, P2tog tbl, P6, P2tog, P25. 58 sts.

Next row: K24, K2tog, K6, skpo, K24. 56 sts.

Next row: P23, P2tog tbl, P6, P2tog, P23. 54 sts.

[6-9: 9-12] months only

Next row (RS): K22, K2tog, K6, skpo, K22. 52 sts.

Next row: P21, P2tog tbl, P6, P2tog, P21. 50 sts.

Next row: K20, K2tog, K6, skpo, K20. 48 sts.

Next row: P19, P2tog tbl, P6, P2tog, P19. 46 sts.

Next row: K18, K2tog, K6, skpo, K18. 44 sts.

Next row: P17, P2tog tbl, P6, P2tog, P17. 42 sts.

[6-9] months only

Next row (RS): K16, K2tog, K6, skpo, K16. 40 sts.

Next row: P15, P2tog tbl, P6, P2tog, P15. 38 sts.

[3-6] months only

Next row (RS): K18, K2tog, K6, skpo, K18. 44 sts.

Next row: P17, P2tog tbl, P6, P2tog, P17. 42 sts.

Next row: K16, K2tog, K6, skpo, K16. 40 sts.

Next row: P15, P2tog tbl, P6, P2tog, P15. 38 sts.

0-3 [3-6] months only

Next row (RS): K14, K2tog, K6, skpo, K14. 36 sts.

Next row: P13, P2tog tbl, P6, P2tog, P13. 34 sts.

0-3 months only

Next row (RS): K12, K2tog, K6, skpo, K12. 32 sts.

Next row: P11, P2tog tbl, P6, P2tog, P11. 30 sts.

Next row: K10, K2tog, P6, skpo, K10. 28 sts.

Next row: P9: P2tog tbl, P6, P2tog, P9. 26 sts.

All sizes

Cut off yarn.

Shape cuff and front tab

Next row (RS): Sl first 9 [12: 13: 14] sts on a holder (left back) then with RS facing, using US 3 (3.25 mm) needles rejoin yarn **B** and K until there are 8 [10: 12: 14] sts on right needle, turn and leave rem 9 [12: 13: 14] sts on a second holder (right back).
Working on these 8 [10: 12: 14] sts only, work as folls:

Next row (WS): K1, M1, P to last st, M1, K1. 10 [12: 14: 16] sts.

Row 1: Knit.

Row 2: K2, P to last 2 sts, K2.
Rep the last 2 rows 4 [5: 6: 7] times more then row 1 once more, ending with **WS** facing for next row.

Next row: K1, skpo, K to last 3 sts, K2tog, K1.
Rep last row once more, ending with **WS** facing for next row. 6 [8: 10: 12] sts.
BO knitwise (on **WS**). **

Work straps

Joining row (RS): Using US 3 (3.25 mm) needles and yarn **B** CO 16 [17: 20: 23] sts then K across these 16 [17: 20: 23] CO sts (for first strap), with RS facing, work across the 9 [12: 13: 14] sts left on second holder (right back) as folls: K7 [10: 11: 12], skpo then work across the 9 [12: 13: 14] sts from first holder (left back) as folls: K2tog, K7 [10: 11: 12]. 32 [39: 44: 49] sts.

Next row (Buttonhole row) (WS): P16 [22: 24: 26], K11 [12: 15: 18], K2tog, (yo) twice (to make a buttonhole), skpo, K1.

Next row: K2, (K1, K1 tbl into double yo of previous row), K to end.

Next row: P16 [22: 24: 26], K to end.

Next row (RS): BO 14 [15: 18: 21] sts knitwise (1 st on right needle), K to end. 18 [24: 26: 28] sts.

Next row: P to last 2 sts, K2.

Next row: Knit.

Next row: P to last 2 sts, K2.

Next row (RS): CO 14 [15: 18: 21] sts (for second strap), K to end. 32 [39: 44: 49] sts.

Next row (Buttonhole row) (WS): K to last 5 sts, K2tog, (yo) twice (to make a buttonhole), skpo, K1.

Next row: K2, (K1, K1 tbl into double yo of previous row), K to end.

Next row (WS): Knit.
BO knitwise.

RIGHT BOOTIE

Work as given for left bootie from * to ** then work as folls:

Work straps

Joining row (RS): With RS facing, using US 3 (3.25 mm) needles and yarn **B** work across the 9 [12: 13: 14] sts left on second holder (right back) as folls: K7 [10: 11: 12], skpo then work across the 9 [12: 13: 14] sts from first holder (left back) as folls: K2tog, K7 [10: 11: 12], CO 16 [17: 20: 23] sts (for first strap). 32 [39: 44: 49] sts.

Next row (WS): K16 [17: 20: 23], P to end.

Next row (Buttonhole row) (RS): K to last 5 sts, K2tog, (yo) twice (to make a buttonhole), skpo, K1.

Next row: K2, (K1, K1 tbl into double yo of previous row), K12 [13: 16: 19], P to end.

Next row: Knit.

Next row (WS): BO 14 [15: 18: 21] sts knitwise (1 st on right needle), K until there are 2 sts on right needle, P to end. 18 [24: 26: 28] sts.

Next row: Knit.

Next row: K2, P to end.

Next row: Knit.

Next row (WS): CO 14 [15: 18: 21] sts (for second strap), K16 [17: 20: 23] sts (for strap), P to end. 32 [39: 44: 49] sts.

Next row (Buttonhole row) (RS): K to last 5 sts, K2tog, (yo) twice (to make a buttonhole), skpo, K1.

Next row: K2, (K1, K1 tbl into double yo of previous row), K to end.

Next row (RS): Knit.
BO knitwise (on **WS**).

FINISHING

Join row ends and sole edge of each bootie using backstitch or mattress stitch if preferred. Sew on buttons to correspond with buttonholes on straps.

Stripy Shoes

SIZES
0-6 [6-12] months

ABBREVIATIONS
See inside front flap

MATERIALS NEEDED
🧶 **DMC Woolly** (136 yd/125 m per 50g ball)
1 ball of Light Blue (071) **A**
1 ball of White (001) **B**
🧶 US 5 (3.75 mm) needles
🧶 2 x 12 mm buttons

GAUGE (TENSION)
24 sts and 38 rows to 4 in (10 cm) measured over g st using US 5 (3.75 mm) needles.

STRIPE SEQUENCE

Rows 1 to 2: Using yarn **B**.

Rows 3 to 4: Using yarn **A**.
These 4 rows form stripes

SHOES

LEFT SHOE

INSTEP

Using US 5 (3.75 mm) needles and yarn **A** CO 12 sts for toe edge.

Next row (WS): Knit.

Beg with stripe row 1 and work entirely in g st in stripe sequence (see above) throughout as folls:
Work 14 [18] rows, ending with RS facing for next row.
Keeping stripe patt correct, dec 1 st at each end of next 2 rows. 8 sts.
Cut off yarns and leave these rem 8 sts on a holder.

BUTTON BAND

Using US 5 (3.75 mm) needles and yarn **A** CO 12 sts.
Work in g st for 5 rows, ending with **WS** facing for next row.
Cut off yarn and leave these 12 sts on a holder.

BUTTONHOLE BAND

Using US 5 (3.75 mm) needles and yarn **A** CO 26 [28] sts.

Row 1: Knit

Row 2: (buttonhole row): Knit to last 4 sts, K2tog, yo, (to make a buttonhole), K2.

Row 3: Knit.

Row 4: K12, BO 14 [16] sts knitwise. 12 sts.
Rejoin yarn **A** and knit across rem 12 sts, ending with RS facing for next row.

Next row (RS): Knit across 12 sts of buttonhole band, CO 2 sts, pick up and knit 9 [12] sts evenly along right side of instep, knit across 8 sts of instep from holder, pick up and knit 9 [12] sts evenly along left side of instep, CO 2 sts, then knit across 12 sts of button band. 54 [60] sts.
* Work in g st for 5 [7] rows, ending with RS side facing for next row.
Work a further 2 rows in g st, dec 1 st at each end of every row, ending with RS facing for next row. 50 [56] sts.

Shape sole

Next row (RS): K until there are 29 [32] sts on right needle, turn.

Next row: Sl 1, K7, turn.

Next row: Sl 1, K6, K2tog, turn.

Rep the last row until 20 sts rem (6 sts unworked at each side of sole).

Next row: Sl 1, K5, K3tog, turn.

Next row: Sl 1, K4, K3tog, turn.

Next row: Sl 1, K to end.

BO rem 16 sts knitwise marking centre st with a colored thread **.

RIGHT SHOE

INSTEP

Using US 5 (3.75 mm) needles and yarn **A** CO 12 sts for toe edge.

Next row (WS): Knit.
Beg with stripe row 1 and work entirely in g st in stripe sequence (see above) throughout as folls:
Work 14 [18] rows, ending with RS facing for next row.
Keeping stripe patt correct, dec 1 st at each end of next 2 rows. 8 sts.
Cut off yarns and leave these rem 8 sts on a holder.

BUTTONHOLE BAND

Using US 5 (3.75 mm) needles and yarn **A** CO 26 [28] sts.

Row 1: Knit

Row 2: (buttonhole row): K2, yo, K2tog (to make a buttonhole), Knit to end.

Row 3: Knit.

Row 4: BO 14 [16] sts knitwise, K to end. 12 sts.

Row 5: Knit.

Cut off yarn and leave these rem 12 sts on a holder.

BUTTON BAND

Using US 5 (3.75 mm) needles and yarn **A** CO 12 sts.
Work in g st for 5 rows, ending with RS facing for next row.

Next row (RS): Knit across 12 sts of button band, CO 2 sts, pick up and knit 9 [12] sts evenly along right side of instep, knit across 8 sts of instep from holder, pick up and knit 9 [12] sts evenly along left side of instep, CO 2 sts, then knit across 12 sts of buttonhole band. 54 [60] sts.
Now work as given for left shoe from * to **.

FINISHING

Join row ends of each bootie using backstitch or mattress stitch if preferred. Place colored thread to centre back seam and join across to form back edge of heel. Sew on buttons to correspond with buttonholes.

Lace Booties

SIZES
0-6 [6-12] months

ABBREVIATIONS
See inside front flap

MATERIALS NEEDED
🧶 **DMC Woolly** (136 yd/125 m per 50g ball)
1 ball of White (001) **A**
1 ball of Pink (043) **B**
1 ball of Green (081) **C**
🧶 US 5 (3.75 mm) needles
🧶 1 yd (90 cm) of 5mm ribbon

GAUGE (TENSION)
25 sts and 34 rows to 4 in (10 cm) measured over st st using US 5 (3.75 mm) needles.

LEFT BOOTIE

Using US 5 (3.75 mm) needles and yarn **A** CO 29 [35] sts. Beg with a K row, work in st st for 2 rows, ending with RS facing for next row.

Picot row (RS): K1, *yo, K2tog, rep from * to end.
Beg with a P row, work in st st for 3 rows, ending with RS facing for next row.

Row 1 (RS): K5, *yo, skpo, K4, rep from * to end.

Row 2 and every foll alt row: Purl.

Row 3: K3, *K2tog, yo, K1, yo, skpo, K1, rep from * to last 2 sts, K2.

Row 5: K2, K2tog, yo, K3, *yo, sl 1, K2tog, psso, yo, K3, rep from * to last 4 sts, yo, skpo, K2.

Row 7: K4, *yo, sl 1. K2tog, psso, yo, K3, rep from * to last st, K1.

Row 9: As row 1.

Row 10: Purl dec 2 [5] sts evenly across row. 27 [30] sts.

Ribbon row (RS): K2 [0], *K2tog, yo, K1, rep from * to last 1 [0] sts, K1 [0].

Beg with a P row, work in st st for 3 rows, ending with RS facing for next row.

Shape instep

Row 1 (RS): K18 [20], turn.

Row 2: P until there are 9 [10] sts on right needle and turn.

Working on these 9 [10] sts only work as folls:
Beg with a K row, work in st st for 14 [16] rows, ending with RS facing for next row.
Cut off yarn.

With RS facing, using US 5 (3.75 mm) needles and yarn **A**, rejoin to inner edge of first 9 [10] sts, pick up and knit 11 [13] sts evenly along right side of instep, knit across 9 [10] sts of toe, pick up and knit 11 [13] sts evenly along left side of instep and knit across rem 9 [10] sts. 49 [56] sts.
Work in g st for 5 [7] rows, ending with RS facing for next row.

Shape sole

Row 1 (RS): K2, skpo, K17 [20], K2tog, K3 [4], skpo, K17 [20], K2tog, K2. 45 [52] sts.

Row 2 and every foll alt row: Knit.

Row 3: K2, skpo, K15 [18], K2tog, K3 [4], skpo, K15 [18], K2tog, K2. 41 [48] sts.

Row 5: K2, skpo, K13 [16], K2tog, K3 [4], skpo, K13 [16], K2tog, K2. 37 [44] sts.

Row 6: Knit.
BO.

RIGHT BOOTIE

Work as given for left bootie.

FINISHING

Join row ends and sole edge of each bootie using backstitch or mattress stitch if preferred. Fold picot edging to WS and slip stitch in place taking care to match sts. Embroider a flower using yarn **B** in centre of each lace diamond with bullion stitch and chain stitches for leaves using yarn **C** as shown in photograph. Thread ribbon through ribbon row.

Cable Double Strap Booties

SIZES
0-6 [6-12] months

ABBREVIATIONS
See inside front flap

SPECIAL ABBREVIATION
C4F slip next 2 sts onto CN and leave at front of work, K2, then K2 from CN.

MATERIALS NEEDED
✄ **DMC Woolly** (136 yd/125 m per 50g ball)
1 ball of Light Grey (121)
✄ US 5 (3.75 mm) needles
✄ Cable needle
✄ 4 x 12 mm buttons

GAUGE (TENSION)
30 sts and 34 rows to 4 in (10 cm) measured over patt using US 5 (3.75 mm) needles.

LEFT BOOTIE

Using US 5 (3.75 mm) needles CO 43 [52] sts.
Work in g st for 3 rows, ending with **WS** facing for next row.

Next row (buttonhole row) (WS): *K4, Kfb, rep from * to last 13 [17] sts, K9 [13], K2tog, yo, (to make a buttonhole), K2. 49 [59] sts.

Row 1 (RS): K10 [14], P2, *K4, P2, rep from * to last st, K1.

Row 2: P1, *K2, P4, rep from * to last 12 [16] sts, K12 [16].

Row 3: BO 9 [13] sts (1 st on right needle), P2, *C4F, P2, rep from * to last st, K1. 40 [46] sts.

Row 4: P1, *K2, P4, rep from * to last 3 sts, K3, turn and CO 9 [13] sts. 49 [59] sts.

Row 5: As row 1.

Row 6: As row 2.

Row 7: K10 [14], P2, *C4F, P2, rep from * to last st, K1.

Row 8 (buttonhole row) (WS): P1, *K2, P4, rep from * to last 12 [16] sts, K8 [12], K2tog, yo, (to make a buttonhole), K2.

Row 9: As row 1.

Row 10: As row 2.
Row 11: As row 3. 40 [46] sts.

Row 12: P1, K2, *P4, K2, rep from * to last st, P1. Place marker at each end of last row.
* Work leg

Row 1 (RS): K1, P2, *K4, P2, rep from * to last st, K1.

Row 2: P1, K2, *P4, K2, rep from * to last st, P1.

111

Row 3: K1, P2, *C4F, P2, rep from * to last st, K1.

Row 4: As row 14.

These 4 rows form patt.
Cont in patt for a further 5 [9] rows, ending with Row 1 and **WS** facing for next row.

Next row (WS): Knit, dec 9 [10] sts evenly across row. 31 [35] sts.

Shape instep

Row 1 (RS): K21 [24], turn.

Row 2: K until there are 11 [13] sts on right needle and turn.

Working on these 11 [13] sts only work as folls:
Work in g st for 10 [14] rows, ending with RS facing for next row.

Next row (RS): K1, skpo, K to last 3 sts, K2tog, K1.

Next row: Knit.
Rep the last 2 rows once more. 7 [9] sts.
Cut off yarn.

With RS facing, using US 5 (3.75 mm) needles, rejoin yarn to inner edge of first 10 [11] sts, pick up and knit 8 [12] sts evenly along right side of instep, knit across 7 [9] sts of toe, pick up and knit 8 [12] sts evenly along left side of instep and knit across rem 10 [11] sts. 43 [55] sts.
Work in g st for 5 rows, ending with RS facing for next row.

Shape sole

Row 1 (RS): K1, skpo, K14 [20], K2tog, K5, skpo, K14 [20], K2tog, K1. 39 [51] sts.
Row 2 and every foll alt row: Knit.

Row 3: K1, skpo, K13 [19], K2tog, K3, skpo, K13 [19], K2tog, K1. 35 [47] sts.

Row 5: K1, skpo, K12 [18], K2tog, K1, skpo, K12 [18], K2tog, K1. 31 [43] sts.

Row 7: K1, skpo, K11 [17], sl 1, K2tog, psso, K11 [17], K2tog, K1. 27 [39] sts.

Row 8: Knit.
BO **.

RIGHT BOOTIE

Using US 5 (3.75 mm) needles CO 43 [52] sts.
Work in g st for 3 rows, ending with **WS** facing for next row.

Next row (buttonhole row) (WS): K2, yo, K2tog, (to make a buttonhole), K9 [13], *Kfb, K4, rep from * to end. 49 [59] sts.

Row 1 (RS): K1, *P2, K4, rep from * to last 12 [16] sts, P2, K10 [14].

Row 2: K12 [16], *P4, K2 rep from * to last st, P1.
Row 3: K1, *P2, C4F, rep from * to last 12 [16] sts, P2, K10 [14].

Row 4: BO 9 [13] sts knitwise (1 st on right needle), K2, *P4, K2, rep from * to last st, P1. 40 [46] sts.

Row 5: K1, P2, *K4, P2, rep from * to last st, K1, turn and CO 9 [13] sts. 49 [59] sts.

Row 6: As row 2.

Row 7: As row 3.

Row 8: As row 2.

Row 9 (buttonhole row) (RS): K1, P2, *K4, P2, rep from * to last 10 [14] sts, K6 [10], K2tog, yo, (to make a buttonhole), K2.

Row 10: As row 2.

Row 11: As row 3.

Row 12: As row 4. 40 [46] sts. Place marker at each end of last row.

Now work as given for left bootie from * to **.

FINISHING

Join sole edge and row ends as far as markers on each bootie using backstitch or mattress stitch if preferred. Sew on buttons to correspond with buttonholes using photo as a guide.

Two Color Simple Booties

SIZES
0-3 [3-6: 6-9: 9-12] months

ABBREVIATIONS
See inside front flap

MATERIALS NEEDED
- **DMC Woolly** (136 yd/125 m per 50g ball)
1 ball of Olive (091) **A**
1 ball of Blue (075) **B**
- US 3 (3.25 mm) needles
- US 5 (3.75 mm) needles

GAUGE (TENSION)
25 sts and 34 rows to 4 in (10 cm) measured over st st using US 5 (3.75 mm) needles.

LEFT BOOTIE

Using US 3 (3.25 mm) needles and yarn **A** CO 20 [24: 26: 28] sts.

Rows 1, 3, 5 and 7: Knit.

Row 2: K1, M1, K8 [10: 11: 12], M1, K2, M1, K8 [10: 11: 12], M1, K1. 24 [28: 30: 32] sts.

Row 4: K1, M1, K10 [12: 13: 14], M1, K2, M1, K10 [12: 13: 14], M1, K1. 28 [32: 34: 36] sts.

Row 6: K1, M1, K12 [14: 15: 16], M1, K2, M1, K12 [14: 15: 16], M1, K1. 32 [36: 38: 40] sts.

Row 8: K1, M1, K14 [16: 17: 18], M1, K2, M1, K14 [16: 17: 18], M1, K1. 36 [40: 42: 44] sts.

Change to US 5 (3.75 mm) needles and yarn **B**.
Beg with a K row, work in st st for 4 rows, ending with RS facing for next row.

Next row (RS): *Knit tog next st and same stitch 4 rows below (from back of work), rep from * to end.

Next row: P1 [3: 0: 1], Pfb, (P3, Pfb) 8 [8: 10: 10] times, P2 [4: 1: 2]. 45 [49: 53: 55] sts.
Beg with a K row, work in st st for 6 [6: 8: 8] rows, ending with RS facing for next row.

Shape instep

Next row (RS): K25 [27: 30: 31], skpo, turn.

Row 1 (WS): P until there are 6 [6: 8: 8] sts on right needle, P2tog, turn.

Row 2: K until there are 6 [6: 8: 8] sts on right needle, skpo, turn.

Rep last 2 rows until 33 [33: 37: 39] sts rem, ending with RS facing for next row.

Next row (RS): Knit to end of row.

Beg with a P row, work in st st for 5 [5: 7: 7] rows across all sts, ending with RS facing for next row. 33 [33: 37: 39] sts.
Cut off yarn **B** and join on yarn **A**.

Next row (RS): Knit dec 3 [3: 3: 1] sts evenly across row.

30 [30: 34: 38] sts.

Change to US 3 (3.25 mm) needles.

Row 1: K2, *P2, K2, rep from * to end.

Row 2: P2, *K2, P2, rep from * to end.
Last 2 rows form rib.
Work a further 23 [25: 27: 29] rows in rib, ending with row 1.
BO in rib.

RIGHT BOOTIE

Work as given for left bootie.

FINISHING

Join row ends and sole edge of each bootie using backstitch or mattress stitch if preferred, reversing seam for cuff.

Little Bow Shoes

SIZES
0-6 [6-12] months

ABBREVIATIONS
See inside front flap

MATERIALS NEEDED
✎ **DMC Woolly** (136 yd/125 m per 50g ball)
1 ball of Bright Pink (054) **A**
1 ball of Pink (042) **B**
✎ US 3 (3.25 mm) needles
✎ US 5 (3.75 mm) needles
✎ 2 x 15 mm buttons

GAUGE (TENSION)
25 sts and 34 rows to 4 in (10 cm) measured over st st using US 5 (3.75 mm) needles.

LEFT SHOE

Using US 5 (3.75 mm) needles and yarn **A** CO 28 [32] sts.

Row 1 and every foll alt row (RS): Knit.

Row 2: K1, M1, K12 [14], M1, K2, M1, K12 [14], M1, K1. 32 [36] sts.

Row 4: K1, M1, K14 [16], M1, K2, M1, K14 [16], M1, K1. 36 [40] sts.

Row 6: K1, M1, K16 [18], M1, K2, M1, K16 [18], M1, K1. 40 [44] sts.

Row 8: K1, M1, K18 [20], M1, K2, M1, K18 [20], M1, K1. 44 [48] sts.

Row 10: K1, M1, K20 [22], M1, K2, M1, K20 [22], M1, K1. 48 [52] sts, ending with RS facing for next row.
Beg with a K row, work in st st for 4 [6] rows, ending with RS facing for next row.

Shape top of foot

Row 1 (RS): K19 [21], (skpo) twice, K2, (K2tog) twice, K19 [21]. 44 [48] sts.

Row 2: Purl.

Row 3: K17 [19], (skpo) twice, K2, (K2tog) twice, K17 [19]. 40 [44] sts.

Row 4: Purl.

Row 5: K13 [15], (skpo) 3 times, K2, (K2tog) 3 times, K13 [15]. 34 [38] sts.

Row 6: Purl. *

Divide for straps

Next row (RS): K until there are 9 [10] sts on right needle, BO 16 [18] sts **purlwise** (1 st on right needle after BO), place last st on right needle back onto left needle and CO 7 [9] sts, then K to end. 16 [19] sts. Working on these 16 [19] sts only for first side, work as folls:

Next row (buttonhole row) (WS): Knit to last 4 sts, K2tog, yo (to make a buttonhole), K2.

Next row: Knit, ending with **WS** facing for next row. BO knitwise (on **WS**).

With **WS** facing, using US 5 (3.75 mm) needles, rejoin yarn **A** to rem 9 [10] sts and CO 7 [9] sts, K to end. 16 [19] sts.
Work in g st for 2 rows, ending with RS facing for next row.
BO.

RIGHT SHOE

Work as given for left shoe as far as *.

Divide for straps

Next row (RS): K until there are 9 [10] sts on right needle, BO 16 [18] sts **purlwise** (1 st on right needle after BO), place last st on right needle back onto left needle and CO 7 [9] sts, then K to end. 16 [19] sts. Working on these 16 [19] sts only for first side, work as folls:
Work in g st for 2 rows, ending with **WS** facing for next row.
BO knitwise (on **WS**).

With **WS** facing, using US 5 (3.75 mm) needles, rejoin yarn **A** to rem 9 [10] sts and CO 7 [9] sts, K to end. 16 [19] sts.

Next row (buttonhole row) (RS): Knit to last 4 sts, K2tog, yo (to make a buttonhole), K2.
Next row: Knit, ending with RS facing for next row. BO.

BOWS (make 2)

Using US 3 (3.25 mm) needles and yarn **B** CO 17 sts. Work in g st for 7 rows, ending with **WS** facing for next row.
BO knitwise (on **WS**).

FINISHING

Join row ends and sole edge of each shoe using backstitch or mattress stitch if preferred. Using a length of yarn **B** wrap yarn tightly around centre strip of bow to form a bow shape, then sew to centre of each shoe as shown in photograph. Sew on buttons to correspond with buttonholes.

Stripy Picot Socks

SIZES
0-6 [6-12] months

ABBREVIATIONS
See inside front flap

MATERIALS NEEDED
🧶 **DMC Woolly** (136 yd/125 m per 50g ball)
1 ball of Bright Pink (054) **A**
1 ball of Orange (102) **B**
1 ball of Turquoise (074) **C**
🧶 US 3 (3.25 mm) needles
🧶 US 5 (3.75 mm) needles
🧶 Stitch holders

GAUGE (TENSION)
25 sts and 34 rows to 4 in (10 cm) measured over st st using US 5 (3.75 mm) needles.

STRIPE SEQUENCE

Rows 1 and 2: Using yarn **A**.

Rows 3 and 4: Using yarn **B**.
These 4 rows form stripe sequence and are repeated throughout.

LEFT SOCK

Using US 3 (3.25 mm) needles and yarn **A** *CO 4 sts, BO 2 sts (1 st on right needle), slip the st on right needle onto left needle, rep from * until there are 26 [32] sts on left needle, then CO 1 st. 27 [33] sts.

Change to yarn **B**.

Row 1 (RS): K1, *P1, K1, rep from * to end.

Row 2: P1, *K1, P1, rep from * to end.
These 2 rows form rib.

Cont in rib for a further 4 rows, dec 1 st at end of last row and ending with RS facing for next row. 26 [32] sts.

Change to US 5 (3.75 mm) needles.
Beg with stripe row 1 and a K row, now work in st st in stripe sequence (see above) throughout as folls:
Work 12 [16] rows of stripe patt, ending with RS facing for next row.

Divide sts for heel

Row 1 (RS): Sl first 7 [9] sts on a holder, using yarn **A** knit 12 [14], slip these 12 [14] sts on a second holder for instep, using yarn **C** knit the rem 7 [9] sts on left needle then knit across the 7 [9] sts from first holder. 14 [18] sts.

Working on these 14 [18] sts only for heel and yarn **C** beg with a P row, work 5 [7] rows in st st, ending with RS facing for next row.

Turn heel

Row 1 (RS): K8 [10], skpo, turn.

Row 2: sl 1, P2, P2tog, turn.

Row 3: sl 1, K3, skpo, turn.

Row 4: sl 1, P4, P2tog, turn.

Row 5: sl 1, K5, skpo, turn.

0-6 months only

Row 6 (WS): sl 1, P6, P2tog. 8 sts.

[6-12] months only

Row 6 (WS): sl 1, P6, P2tog, turn. 10 sts.

Row 7: sl 1, K7, skpo, turn. 9 sts.

Row 8: sl 1, P8, P2tog. 8 sts.

For all sizes

Cut off yarn and sl these rem 8 sts on a holder.
With RS facing, using US 5 (3.75 mm) needles and yarn **A**, pick up and knit 6 [8] sts along side of heel, knit across 8 sts on holder, then pick up and knit 6 [8] sts along other side of heel. 20 [24] sts.

Next row (WS): Purl.

Shape sole

Keeping stripe patt correct, work as folls:

Row 1 (RS): K1 skpo, K to last 3 sts, K2tog, K1. 18 [22] sts.

Row 2: Purl.

Keeping stripe patt correct, dec 1 st at each end as before on next and every foll alt row until 12 [14] sts rem, then work 11 [13] rows straight in stripe patt. Cut off yarns.

Shape toe

Using yarn **C** only.

Row 1 (RS): K1, skpo, K to last 3 sts, K2tog, K1. 10 [12] sts.

Row 2: Purl.
Rep last 2 rows until 6 [8] sts rem, ending with RS facing for next row.
BO.

Instep

With **WS** facing, using US 5 (3.75 mm) needles and yarn **A**, purl across 12 [14] sts left on a holder.
Keeping stripe patt correct, work 18 [22] rows straight, ending with RS facing for next row.
Cut off yarns.

Shape toe

Using yarn **C** only.

Row 1 (RS): K1, skpo, K to last 3 sts, K2tog, K1. 10 [12] sts.

Row 2: Purl.
Rep last 2 rows until 6 [8] sts rem, ending with RS facing for next row.
BO.

RIGHT SOCK

Work as given for left sock.

FINISHING

Join row ends at back, side edges then across toe edge using backstitch or mattress stitch if preferred, taking care to match patt.

Bell Edging Socks

SIZES
0-6 [6-12] months

ABBREVIATIONS
See page ??

MATERIALS NEEDED
🧶 **DMC Woolly** (136 yd/125 m per 50g ball)
1 ball of Pink (042)
🧶 US 3 (3.25 mm) needles
🧶 US 5 (3.75 mm) needles
🧶 Stitch holders

GAUGE (TENSION)
25 sts and 34 rows to 4 in (10 cm) measured over st st using US 5 (3.75 mm) needles.

LEFT SOCK

Using US 5 (3.75 mm) needles CO 57 [73] sts.

Row 1 (RS): P2, K5, *P3, K5, rep from * to last 2 sts, P2.

Row 2: K2, P5, *K3, P5, rep from * to last 2 sts, K2.
Rep last 2 rows once more.

Row 5: P2, skpo, K1, K2tog, *P3, skpo, K1, K2tog, rep from * to last 2 sts, P2. 43 [55] sts.

Row 6: K2, P3, *K3, P3, rep from * to last 2 sts, K2.

Row 7: P2, sl 2, K1, psso, *P3, sl 2, K1, psso, rep from * to last 2 sts, P2. 29 [37].

Row 8: K2tog, P1, *K3, P1, rep from * to last 2 sts, K2tog. 27 [35] sts.

Change to US 3 (3.25 mm) needles.

Row 1 (RS): P1, *K1, P1, rep from * to end.

Row 2: K1, *P1, K1, rep from * to end.
These 2 rows form rib.
Cont in rib for a further 5 rows ending with RS facing for next row.

Change to US 5 (3.75 mm) needles.

Next row (RS): Knit, dec 1 [3] sts evenly across row. 26 [32] sts.

Beg with a P row, now work in st st for 11 [15] rows, ending with RS facing for next row. Cut off yarn.

Divide sts for heel

Row 1 (RS): Sl first 7 [9] sts on a holder, rejoin yarn and knit 12 [14], slip these 12 [14] sts on a second holder for instep, knit the rem 7 [9] sts on left needle then knit across the 7 [9] sts from first holder. 14 [18] sts.

Working on these 14 [18] sts only for heel and beg with a P row, work 5 [7] rows in st st, ending with RS facing for next row.

Turn heel

Row 1 (RS): K8 [10], skpo, turn.

Row 2: sl 1, P2, P2tog, turn.

Row 3: sl 1, K3, skpo, turn.

Row 4: sl 1, P4, P2tog, turn.

Row 5: sl 1, K5, skpo, turn.

0-6 months only

Row 6 (WS): sl 1, P6, P2tog. 8 sts.

[6-12] months only

Row 6 (WS): sl 1, P6, P2tog, turn. 10 sts.

Row 7: sl 1, K7, skpo, turn. 9 sts.

Row 8: sl 1, P8, P2tog. 8 sts.

For all sizes

Cut off yarn and sl these rem 8 sts on a holder.
With RS facing, using US 5 (3.75 mm) needles, pick up and knit 6 [8] sts along side of heel, knit across 8 sts on holder, then pick up and knit 6 [8] sts along other side of heel. 20 [24] sts.

Next row (WS): Purl.

Shape sole

Row 1 (RS): K1 skpo, K to last 3 sts, K2tog, K1. 18 [22] sts.

Row 2: Purl.

Dec 1 st at each end as before on next and every foll alt row until 12 [14] sts rem, ending with WS facing for next row.
Beg with a P row, work in st st for 11 [13] rows, ending with RS facing for next row.

Shape toe

Row 1 (RS): K1, skpo, K to last 3 sts, K2tog, K1. 10 [12] sts.

Row 2: Purl.

Rep last 2 rows until 6 [8] sts rem, ending with RS facing for next row.
BO.

Instep

With **WS** facing, using US 5 (3.75 mm) needles, purl across 12 [14] sts left on a holder.
Beg with a K row, work 18 [22] rows in st st, ending with RS facing for next row.

Shape toe

Row 1 (RS): K1, skpo, K to last 3 sts, K2tog, K1. 10 [12] sts.

Row 2: Purl.

Rep last 2 rows until 6 [8] sts rem, ending with RS facing for next row.
BO.

RIGHT SOCK

Work as given for left sock.

FINISHING

Join row ends at back, reversing seam for cuff, then, side edges and across toe edge using backstitch or mattress stitch if preferred.